CAMBRIDGE LIBRARY COLLECTION

Books of enduring scholarly value

Women's Writing

The later twentieth century saw a huge wave of academic interest in women's writing, which led to the rediscovery of neglected works from a wide range of genres, periods and languages. Many books that were immensely popular and influential in their own day are now studied again, both for their own sake and for what they reveal about the social, political and cultural conditions of their time. A pioneering resource in this area is Orlando: Women's Writing in the British Isles from the Beginnings to the Present (http://orlando.cambridge.org), which provides entries on authors' lives and writing careers, contextual material, timelines, sets of internal links, and bibliographies. Its editors have made a major contribution to the selection of the works reissued in this series within the Cambridge Library Collection, which focuses on non-fiction publications by women on a wide range of subjects from astronomy to biography, music to political economy, and education to prison reform.

Notes and Sketches of New South Wales

Louisa Anne Meredith (1812–95) had published poetry, journalism, and books on flowers before emigrating from England to Australia in 1839. Her 1844 account of the journey there and of her early impressions of the people was somewhat derogatory, and caused considerable offence in Sydney, although the book was widely read both in Australia and in England. However, her lyrical descriptions of nature were extremely popular, and she was also a talented illustrator of her own work. She published some twenty books, and many other writings, making her one of the most commercially successful women writers in Australia. Her *My Home in Tasmania* (1852) is also reprinted in this series. Her books remain valuable as a source of information on the social history of Australia in the mid nineteenth century, and also on natural history. For more information on this author, see http://orlando.cambridge.org/public/svPeople?person_id=merelo

Cambridge University Press has long been a pioneer in the reissuing of out-of-print titles from its own backlist, producing digital reprints of books that are still sought after by scholars and students but could not be reprinted economically using traditional technology. The Cambridge Library Collection extends this activity to a wider range of books which are still of importance to researchers and professionals, either for the source material they contain, or as landmarks in the history of their academic discipline.

Drawing from the world-renowned collections in the Cambridge University Library, and guided by the advice of experts in each subject area, Cambridge University Press is using state-of-the-art scanning machines in its own Printing House to capture the content of each book selected for inclusion. The files are processed to give a consistently clear, crisp image, and the books finished to the high quality standard for which the Press is recognised around the world. The latest print-on-demand technology ensures that the books will remain available indefinitely, and that orders for single or multiple copies can quickly be supplied.

The Cambridge Library Collection will bring back to life books of enduring scholarly value (including out-of-copyright works originally issued by other publishers) across a wide range of disciplines in the humanities and social sciences and in science and technology.

Notes and Sketches of New South Wales

During a Residence in that Colony from 1839 to 1844

Louisa Anne Meredith

CAMBRIDGE UNIVERSITY PRESS

Cambridge, New York, Melbourne, Madrid, Cape Town, Singapore,
São Paolo, Delhi, Dubai, Tokyo, Mexico City

Published in the United States of America by Cambridge University Press, New York

www.cambridge.org
Information on this title: www.cambridge.org/9781108024174

This edition first published 1844
This digitally printed version 2010

ISBN 978-1-108-02417-4 Paperback

NOTES AND SKETCHES

OF

NEW SOUTH WALES,

DURING

A RESIDENCE IN THAT COLONY FROM 1839 TO 1844.

BY

MRS. CHARLES MEREDITH.

———

LONDON:

JOHN MURRAY, ALBEMARLE STREET.

———

1844.

LONDON:
Printed by WILLIAM CLOWES and SONS,
Stamford Street.

TO THOSE DEAR ENGLISH FRIENDS FOR WHOSE AMUSEMENT,

AND AT WHOSE REQUEST, THE FOLLOWING PAGES HAVE BEEN

WRITTEN, THEY ARE AFFECTIONATELY INSCRIBED,

BY

LOUISA ANNE MEREDITH.

PREFACE.

I WOULD fain deprecate the censure of severe critics, which the superficial character of the following pages might otherwise call forth, by a few words of explanation as to my motives and objects in publishing them.

Knowing that very many persons at "Home" are deeply interested in these distant Colonies, as being the residence of dear friends and relatives, and that, as in the case of my own home-connexions, they really understand very little of the general aspect of things here, I believed that a few simple sketches from nature, however devoid of scientific lore, would be a welcome addition to the present small fund of information on common every-day topics relating to these antipodean climes; and of such belief, this little work is the result.

My aim has been simply to give my own impressions of whatever appeared worthy observation. I cannot for a moment flatter myself with the idea of conveying information to those skilled in scientific detail; my desire was to give true and general descriptions of scenery, people, and the various objects which strike a new-comer as novel or remarkable; just, in fact, as they appeared to myself. I have sketched every-day things with a faithful and homely pencil; and if the learned find nothing new in my unvarnished narrative, let them not condemn the unambitious attempt to amuse and interest the general, and more especially the young reader. Books of reference I have none, nor can I here obtain the use of any. My own observation, aided by my husband's long experience in these Colonies, is my sole resource; therefore, however defective may be the finish of my picture in detail, the outline is at least original.

As it is necessarily impossible that I can correct the press myself, numerous typographical errors are almost unavoidable, and for which I can only entreat the kind indulgence of my readers.

Spring Vale,
Great Swanport, Van Diemen's Land,
December, 1843.

CONTENTS.

CHAPTER VI.

CHAPTER VII.

CHAPTER VIII.

CHAPTER IX.

CHAPTER X.

CHAPTER XI.

CHAPTER XII.

CHAPTER XIII.

CHAPTER XIV.

CHAPTER XV.

CHAPTER XVI.

NOTES AND SKETCHES,

&c.   &c.

CHAPTER I.

Embarkation—Indisposition—Pleasures of a Sea Voyage—Fellow-passengers
—Observance of Character—Devonshire Coast—Pilots—Land Luxuries—
H.M.S. *Hercules*—Eddystone Lighthouse—Last Land.

EARLY in the month of June, 1839, we left England for New
South Wales; and although at the time the voyage seemed to
me very monotonous and devoid of incident, yet, in writing
any account of the interesting objects these colonies present, I
cannot pass altogether silently over the events, however few or
trifling, that served in some measure to vary the tedium of a four
months' passage hither, which I can assure my readers is far
more irksome than any one would imagine who has not endured
that unpleasant captivity.

It is now more than three years since that time, but I remember most vividly my feelings of disgust on stepping from the
chair in which I was hoisted on board the *Letitia*, amidst the
strange mêlée on deck. I was too ignorant of nautical matters
to make proper allowance for the slovenly aspect of things in
their then incomplete state of arrangement.

Dirt and confusion seemed to share the sovereignty between
them, and the heterogeneous assemblage of trunks, chests, cases,
bags, hampers, hen-coops, pigs, dogs, coils of rope, sailors and
passengers on deck, made me gladly retreat to our own cabin,
where the final disposal of our various goods and chattels occupied
us the remainder of the evening.

B

I was greatly amused and puzzled by Mr. Meredith's extreme caution in lashing every article with ropes to the sides of the cabin, as well as by having deep cleats of wood nailed to the floor to keep our chest of drawers, &c. in place. Even my dressing-case and work-box were tied fast, like a couple of terrible wild animals, lest they should make a sudden rush at us, and the candlestick was securely confined in their company. A convenient shelf, with a strong rail in front, formed an excellent bookcase; and by the time our various little arrangements were completed, our apartment, which was considered a most spacious one, being eight or nine feet square, began to look more snug and habitable than I had believed possible.

Having a stern-cabin, we had the advantage of half the skylight and two stern-windows, which enabled us to enjoy more air and light, and be less annoyed by unpleasant odours, than in any other part of the vessel.

Contrary winds rendered our progress very slow for some days, and that miserable visitation, sea-sickness, kept me almost wholly in my berth, where I lay wearily listening to the novel and strange noises all around me, and hearing with some impatience of our repeated approaches to the French coast, as we slowly beat down the Channel.

To a novice at sea, every hour, nay, every moment, brings some greater or less misery. Even in comparatively still weather, the motion of the vessel, however slight, seems almost intolerable, and you helplessly roll from side to side of your narrow berth, with many a thump and bruise—the best preventive of the latter being a pretty tight wedge, consisting of a desk or box, and pillows. You watch the swing; tray, cloaks, towels, or whatever else is hung up in the cabin, performing various extraordinary gyrations, that make you most unpleasantly giddy as you contemplate the extempore waltzing party, enlivened perhaps by the gentle melody of a couple of sailors holy-stoning the deck overhead, and you are fain to believe your discomfort at its height; but be not too sanguine; skylights *will* sometimes have broken panes, and "bull's-eyes"* are notoriously apt to be leaky, in either of which

---

* Thick glasses inserted in a ship's deck to light the cabins, and favourite spots for people to stand upon when you are reading below.

cases your toilet, such as it is, or your bed, becomes saturated with dirty salt-water. Perhaps a cup of some inexplicable sea-compound, called, by a stretch of courtesy, tea or coffee, is brought to you, and, with the most laudable intention of convey-ing it to your lips, you feel a sudden jerk, and perceive an empty cup fast grasped in your trembling hands, and find that its former contents are communicating an agreeable warmth and moisture to your feet, not much to the improvement of the white counter-pane, but greatly to the diversion of your more experienced com-panion, who, with provoking coolness, inquires, " Why do you pour your breakfast down there ?"

At length, with a heroism not to be lightly appreciated, you resolve to have done playing the invalid, and to go on deck; in an agony of fear, and great dubiousness respecting the relative positions of horizontal and perpendicular, you perform a pain-ful toilet, and may be considered fortunate in escaping any serious hurt. The extraordinary activity of all inanimate articles is a great annoyance and puzzle for a while ; nothing can stand still where you put it. Every comb and brush seems possessed, going jumping about in the most inconvenient manner the moment you require them, and are nearly certain to hop into some impossible corner, as though on purpose to perplex their distressed and un-steady owner in the recovery. When, after all these trials, you cautiously open the door, prepared to make a resolute sally to the " companion" stairs, ten to one but some unlucky bucket, lantern, or other obstacle, lies in wait to embarrass your waver-ing steps ; or a sudden lurch of the ship plunges you headlong into that singular combination of unpleasantnesses, the steward's pan-try ! At length, faint and bewildered, you gain the deck, and sink down on the first resting-place you see, glad to feel the fresh invigorating breeze, and enjoy the clear cheering sunshine. Such at least were my own feelings on this my first voyage, and I doubt not that most novices have a like ordeal of the uncom-fortable to pass through.

As soon as I began to recover, and take a glance around, there were the faces and aspects of our fellow-passengers to be perused with something of anxiety, as it is a point of no trivial import-ance on such a voyage, that the few persons with whom you can associate, and with whom you cannot avoid coming in daily con-

tact for four months, should at least be companionable. I cannot
conceive any situation in life more favourable to the exposure of
real characters and dispositions than a long voyage. Assumed
manners of refinement, counterfeit blandness and courtesy, and,
in fact, every species and form of affectation, are insensibly for-
gotten. Those who are really ill-tempered, find so much for their
humour to feed on, that the surly countenance remains uncontra-
dicted by the soft and obsequious manner; the truly vulgar are
too much engrossed by dear self to seek the favour of others by
pretended refinement; and the harmless little arts of " pretty
virginities," finding how vain is the hope of stimulating to admiration beings whose every faculty and thought are engrossed
by their own petty distresses, are fain to reserve their efforts
for a more favourable season. But when all the counterfeits
have lost their gilding, the true metal is the precious coin still ;
and how valuable in so narrow a circle is unfeigned good-temper,
and that only true politeness which springs from kindness of
heart, none will perfectly understand who have not had specimens
of both kinds in their " compagnons de voyage."

We were fortunate in being able to select a very pleasant circle
from the small community on board, as one by one they shook
off the prevalent indisposition, and reduced their unhappy, pale,
elongated faces to their wonted fair proportions.

When I came on deck on the 8th day of our voyage, I found
we were running along the Devonshire coast before a light breeze,
under as bright a blue sky as ever made England look thrice
lovely in the eyes of those who were leaving her, perhaps for ever.
Many vessels which, like ourselves, had been detained by the
adverse winds, were now in sight, their white wing-like sails
fairly spread, and taking all advantage of the welcome change.
Sea-gulls swept majestically by, their arched and outspread wings
glancing brightly in the sunlight, and their easy, graceful
motion seeming a scornful reproach to the unsteady awkward
movements of such novices at sea as myself. As we neared
Plymouth, where we had to put in for some passengers, a pilot
came on board, and the careless yet secure activity with which
he sprang from his boat up the ship's side and on deck seemed
worthy of Ducrow himself, unable as I was to go three steps
without holding on by something.

I felt quite a respect for that bronzed weather-beaten seaman, as I thought of the inestimable services he and his fellows, the Channel pilots, render both to our own and foreign shipping. In rough or foggy weather, when vessels ignorant of the difficult navigation of the Channel would, but for their guidance, be inevitably lost, they are out in their boats braving such seas, that it does seem almost miraculous such mere boats can live in them. But however stormy the weather or dark the night, there are the pilots ready at the known signal to run alongside and leap upon the stranger's deck. They are most brave and gallant fellows, and many a good ship owes to them the lives of her crew and the safety of her rich freight.

We entered Plymouth Sound in the evening, and for the last time watched the sun set on English hills and woods. I felt as if to set foot on land only for a few minutes would be the greatest imaginable treat ; but we cast anchor so late, that I was compelled to forego the pleasure, and sat on deck watching the boats as they went ashore, thinking their passengers must be almost too happy. A late repast of fresh bread, clean, land-made bread, fresh butter, strawberries, and clouted cream, however, almost consoled me for my previous disappointment. A lucky mortal, permitted to taste the ambrosia of the Gods, would not find it half so delicious as would a poor sea-sick creature, a victim to the unknown atrocious compounds of a dirty black sea-steward, think such a feast as mine !

We were up and on deck early the following morning, unwilling to lose a minute's view of the beautiful scenery around. A man-of-war, the *Hercules*, lying in the harbour, sent a boat to reconnoitre our crew, greatly to the discomfort and apprehension of our captain, but fortunately without depriving him of any " hands." I listened to the morning music on board the *Hercules*, and thought that our grand national air, " Rule Britannia," much as I ever admired it, never sounded so beautiful as then ; and I wept to think I should perhaps never more hear it in my own beloved native land.

We weighed anchor between six and seven o'clock, and in passing the *Hercules* made a polite nautical salutation, by lowering our royals (an obeisance always expected by ships of war from the humbler body of merchantmen) ; and the officer on duty ordered the band aft to give us a cheering and melodious farewell as we left the harbour.

We had a fine view for some time of the lovely shores of Devon, and of that noble effort of human science and perseverance, the Eddystone Lighthouse. How mean and contemptible, beside such a fabric, erected for so great and good a purpose, seem by comparison the mere gewgaw palaces of luxury and ostentation, so profusely scattered over our fair country! and yet how few, how very few erections of a like kind are there, inestimable as is their value in the saving of human *life*, to say nothing of less precious matters!*

A short time before sunset I went below, intending to return on deck and watch the *last land* fade on the horizon, but on my coming to look for it, an envious bank of clouds hung over the spot, and totally hid it. Some one began singing, " Isle of Beauty, fare thee well !"—had they *felt* half as much as I did, they could not have uttered a single note.

---

* Why was not the " Nelson Monument" a Lighthouse? I can conceive no fabric of more grandeur and costliness half so acceptable to the spirit it is designed to honour, as the humblest erection devoted to such a service.

CHAPTER II.

Bay of Biscay—Spanish Coast—Employment the best preventive of Ennui—
Phosphorescence of the Sea—Portuguese Men-of-War—Swallows—Tene-
riffe— Speaking the *Cherub*—Fear of Pirates—Porpoises—Flying-Fish
—Capture of a Boneto—Dolphins.

WE were now fairly "at sea," with no chance of any *pleasant*
variety of scene, as, unluckily for us, our "good ship Argo" was
to make a direct passage to Sydney, without touching at any
intermediate port. Like true philosophers, we consoled ourselves
by the reflection that, as some compensation for the disappointment, our voyage would be the more speedy from having no in-
terruption ; though to sail half round the world, and be *near* so
many interesting and beautiful spots, of which I had heard and
read so much, and not to see even one of them—not Madeira, with
its vine-clad hills—nor Teneriffe, nor even the Cape, that general "half-way house" for poor exiles like ourselves—certainly
appeared rather hard, and, as I considered it, great waste of time
and travelling.

The Bay of Biscay, so renowned in song and story for its
stormy winds and waves, was happily in a most pacific mood
when we crossed it with a fair light breeze and sunny weather ;
and though the fine old song was often quoted at the time, *we*
had no disastrous consequences to remind us

> " Of the day
> When we lay
> In the Bay of Biscay O !"

We "sighted" the Spanish and Portuguese coasts, and with
glasses could discern trees and white houses or cottages ; and as
wishful imagination converted every green thing into an orangery
or a vineyard, our distant gazes made us still more anxious for a
nearer investigation of the good things we fancied there. But
the inexorable ship sailed on, and hills, vineyards, and cottages
faded into mist again.

I passed every day on deck, busy with that most pleasant of all
"fancy-work," wool embroidery; and to it I owe my exemption
from much of the overpowering ennui so general on a long voyage. To *study* is, I think, impossible, and I very soon disposed
of all the light reading to be found on board, when compelled by
illness or bad weather to remain below. But my work-basket
and frame were my daily companions, and I was often told how
enviable was my happiness in having something to employ me.

Many evenings we spent in watching the beautiful phosphoric
appearance of the sea after dark, and trying to reconcile the
various theories advanced by naturalists respecting it. That
it is caused by floating animalcula is the general opinion; but if
so, they must be as innumerable as motes in the sunshine, or as
grains of sand upon the sea-shore, else how are the myriad millions of glittering lights to be accounted for that sparkle in a
single wave? Some are much larger and brighter than the rest,
bearing about the same proportion to each other as do stars of
the first and sixth magnitude, and these larger points may, by
close watching, be traced for several seconds, whilst the smaller
ones flash and disappear simultaneously. I know of nothing to
which I can compare this most beautiful and wonderful appearance, unless I have recourse to Sindbad's Diamond Valley, and
beg you to fancy millions of millions of jewel-sparks, and a few
thousands of larger brilliants, all rapidly whirling and glancing
in one vivid glittering mass: but even diamonds would not shine
alone in a dark night, so *that* simile will not do. The bright
creatures—if creatures they are—do not seem to extend far down
into the sea, because I have observed, in looking over the stern,
that *immediately* following the rudder there always remained a
small dark space beyond which the separated waves full of lights
united again, and formed a long bright pathway on the water in
the wake of the ship. The phosphoric lights seemed roused to
life by the passage of the vessel through them; a fish swimming
past produced the same effect on a smaller scale; a bucket of
water from the brightest part lost all the glittering appearance
almost instantly when hoisted on deck. The colour of the lights
was bluish, or just what a purely white light would be, seen
through the blue water. Perhaps the spray of a "jet d'eau,"
seen in a strong moonlight, would give the best idea of this most

indescribable phenomenon.   I was never weary of watching it,
and often, after leaving my usual evening-seat by the taffrail,
could not help returning again and again for one more dazzled,
earnest gaze.

I first saw those curious and beautiful little animals the Portuguese men-of-war, *Physalus pelagicus* of naturalists, in about
36° N. lat., and for many days they were very numerous, robbing
my work of nearly all my attention in gazing at their elegant
forms and colours.   I had a few caught, to examine them more
closely.   They consist of a flat, thin, transparent membrane,
from one and a half to two inches long, of an oval shape; and on
the upper side of this, down the centre, runs a similar membrane
standing erect, at right angles with the flat one.   A whole wafer
laid on the table, and the half of another placed edgewise upon
it (the straight side downwards, of course), will give some idea
of the form of the animal, or rather of the tiny ship's deck and
sail.   The under part is furnished with several rows of tentacula
spreading out like a beautiful flower, varying in colour in different specimens, and sometimes even in one, through many shades
of blue, pink, and soft purple.   A slight coloured film also enve-
lops the transparent membrane above described, giving it a beautiful iridescent appearance when sailing along in the sunshine.
By putting them in a basin of sea-water, I was enabled to keep
and observe them for some time ; but when taken out of their
natural element, the delicate tentacula shrink and dissolve away
very soon ; though with care the thin glassy membrane with its
fragile sail may be permanently preserved by drying.

Their method of navigation is not the least interesting point to
notice in these fairy-mariners.   I have frequently observed one
sailing complacently along, his arms, like the many oars of an
ancient galley, spread around him, and his delicate glassy sail
set full to the breeze ; when a sudden puff of wind has overset
him altogether, and plunged the whole fabric under water : the
next instant he is up again as gay as before, but at first only
presents his sail *edgewise* to the wind, and then seems to tack
about very cautiously, as if to try how much canvas he can
carry in safety.   This *may* not be really the case, but I have
watched many do exactly as I describe, and must therefore believe in their nautical skill.   Like other creatures of their class,

they no doubt feed on minute mollusca and animalcula, which they entrap in their numerous tentacula, or arms.   Their lower side very much resembles some of the beautiful sea anemones* so common on rocks covered at high-water on this coast,† and, from what I remember, there are similar ones on those of England.‡

Some poor little swallows, apparently worn out with fatigue, alighted on the rigging one day, and hovered about the ship. The sailors caught and tried to feed some of them ; and one that flew into our cabin through the stern-window, I endeavoured to tempt with soaked biscuit, crumbs, and water, but could not prevail on my poor little patient to eat anything.   I left him alone, hoping he would grow more assured, but he escaped, and was found lying dead on the deck a day or two after.   I imagine the poor birds had either been blown off the land, or, having been baffled by contrary winds in their migratory voyage, had become too much exhausted to fly any farther : no doubt many thousands of them must perish at sea from similar causes.   I have heard Mr. Meredith mention that on his voyage home (to England) in 1838, a beautiful little bird, of a species he was quite unacquainted with, flew on board the ship, and fed greedily on soaked biscuit; *so* greedily indeed, forgetting the needful precautions to be observed by starving people, that he literally died from repletion.

Finding we should pass tolerably near Teneriffe, I became extremely anxious for a good day-view of the Peak, and only feared sailing by in the night and losing it.   We certainly passed by day, about midway between Teneriffe and the " Great Canary," but the mountain was thickly veiled in clouds, nearly to the

---

* *Actinia anemone*, or *Actinia calendula*, probably.
† Oyster Bay, Van Diemen's Land.
‡ I believe De Blainville mentions six species of Physalus; and from having seen descriptions of *P. pelagicus* differing in many points from my own observation of the animal, I am induced to believe that various species are described as the same by different persons.   In the ' Tasmanian Journal of Science,' a paper (by A. Sinclair, Esq., Surgeon, R. N.) descriptive of a *Physalus pelagicus*, mentions, among other features I did not observe in it, the property of stinging severely, possessed by the tentacula, and retained even after the animal has been dried; also that the water in which it had floated had caused violent pain and inflammation in the hands and arms of two boys employed to wash out the tub.   As I repeatedly handled the specimens I had caught, both before and after death, and received no injury, there must be an essential difference in the species.

water's edge, so that a mere shoal or sandbank had been as fine an object. If I could only have seen the merest point of the summit, I had not cared ; I sat " like (im-)patience on a monument," wailing for one clear loophole in those gloomy morose clouds, but in vain—and I still have to take on credit all the grand and inflated descriptions of other more fortunate travellers.

As I did not at the time think I should ever require any memoranda of our monotonous voyage, I kept no regular " log-book," or journal, which now I much regret, as I am without exact data for many occurrences. About the beginning of July we spoke a homeward-bound vessel, the *Cherub*, and gladly availed ourselves of the opportunity to send letters home. The prudent ones had all letters ready written, but I confess I was not one of that number, and a few hurried words of love and greeting were all the homeward-bound *Cherub* bore from me.

There is something peculiarly grand, and withal touching, in that meeting of ships on the wide ocean. People who never heard of each other before, who might live in the same street of the same city for years without knowing each other's face, thus meeting on that trackless highway of the world, the sea, look on one another as if some mysterious communion between them were at once established. I do not mean individually, but generally, for, although I might not accurately observe the face of any one human being on board that vessel, yet I felt as if they were *friends* whom we had met ; and as she afterwards went on *her* way, and we on ours, I looked after her lessening sails with real regret.

After being for days and weeks at sea without any object to break the line of the horizon, that seems to shut in the same eternal circle of water, it is absolutely a treat, an indescribable delight to the eye, to see so beautiful an object as a vessel in full sail gradually nearing, and so occupying a greater portion of the wearisome sea-view. Everything about her is busily discussed, and not unfrequently the inexperienced are gravely informed that she is an " ill-looking craft," " a rakish-looking brig," " very much the cut of a privateer," &c., and mysterious hints are given about muskets, cutlasses, and ammunition, till the well-known ensign with its union-jack is seen spreading to the breeze as they hoist it on board the stranger, and in reply to " Ship ahoy !

What ship's that ?" a gruff English accent, made thrice gruffer
and rougher by bawling into a speaking-trumpet, informs you
that the suspicious craft is the *Mary* or *Betsey*, or some
other good old household name, of London or Liverpool, bound
from ————; whereupon the captain of our ship returns a
like series of explanations, latitudes and longitudes are compared,
and the interview closes.

As we neared the line, I confess I used to pay most especial
attention to the various conjectures raised on the approach of a
strange sail, especially if those learned in such matters seemed
suspicious of her aspect or manœuvres; but I am most happy to
say I have no thrilling narratives of fearful engagements or
providential escapes to relate, as we were never molested by any
of the piratical fraternity. This was fortunate, as our ship, like
most merchantmen, carried her guns snugly and securely stowed
away in the hold along with her cargo; which arrangement,
though doubtless originating in a praiseworthy care of her means
of defence, was not exactly calculated to facilitate the use of them,
had it been needed. A few rusty muskets, and some pistols of
most pacific temperaments, were ostentatiously ranged round the
mizen-mast in the mess-cabin; but, like the broken teacups on
the alehouse chimney-piece, were, I fear, only " kept for show."

Porpoises were a frequent source of amusement to me; for I
exceedingly enjoy watching their ponderous gaiety as they leap
and flounce about, and the agility with which they bound out of
the water is most astonishing. We often saw them leap as high
as the fore-yard, and I used to think they would fairly alight on
the forecastle; but I fancy they knew better than to trust their
lives and oleaginous bodies to the tender mercies of the sailors,
who would infallibly have despatched and eaten them very
speedily. Prodigious shoals of them often crossed our track,
and might be seen in thousands gambolling as far as their black
bodies were visible above the water. My admiration of their
elephantine frolics became so well known, that if I chanced to
be below when a shoal was seen, I immediately received a mes-
sage informing me of the event, and lost no time in hastening
to see the sport.

What a contrast to the unwieldy monsters I have just mentioned are the elegant little flying-fish (*Exocetus volitans*)!

I had no idea they were so beautiful, having been misled by bad engravings, which represented them as thin, shrivelled, starved-looking things, while in reality they are beautifully proportioned, and quite plump, with shining bluish silvery scales, that flash brightly as they glance in the sun. They are about nine or ten inches long, the pectoral fins, or wings, about six inches, and capable of expanding to about three inches and a half at the broadest part; and from tip to tip, when spread, must measure above twelve inches. The eyes are remarkably large and fine, giving an expression to the head more like the glance of a bird than a fish; "fishy eyes" being proverbially dull and lustreless. Only one fell on board, which was brought to me, and, in justice to the memory of the poor defunct, I must confess that, after preserving his wings and tail, I found his remains very delicate eating.

So many arguments have been held with respect to these curious creatures, as to whether they really *fly*, that is, flutter and turn in the air, or merely leap from the top of one wave to fall on the top of another, that nothing but positive proof could induce me to say a word on the subject. I have attentively observed them rise from the water, flutter their fins rapidly, not unlike a lark when first rising; then sail along a short time, *turn*, at various angles from their course, whether in a breeze or calm; and, after being many seconds in the air, dip again into the sea, preparatory to another flight. I have continually mistaken them for birds, being quite deceived by their fluttering motion, so different from what I should have supposed any fish capable of. Some very eminent naturalists affirm that they can neither turn nor flutter; having *seen* them do both repeatedly, I am greatly inclined to differ from them in opinion, and to suppose that they must have observed these beautiful little creatures under some circumstances which prevented or disguised their real movements.

With all their beauty and accomplishments, the poor little flying-fish seem to lead a most restless and unhappy life. As they swim through the sea, the swift and hungry boneto pursues them with a keen and deadly purpose, seeming quite as well aware as myself of their delicate flavour; the dolphin also wages war against them; and the moment they quit the water to escape these ravenous foes, a voracious sea-bird is nearly sure to pounce upon some of the quivering fugitives.

We were sailing for three days through shoals of boneto, and all kinds of murderous devices were adopted for the capture of some, but to no purpose. Fish-hooks, harpoons, &c., were all in request, and the excitement became extreme, to see shoals of fish all around, darting hither and thither in hundreds, all " fit to eat," as the sailors declared, and none to be got! It was terribly exciting, and figures might be seen in every direction, attired in all imaginable variety of costume, and in more than every imaginable attitude, most perseveringly hurling among and hauling in again their innocent weapons. At last, Mr. Meredith, who had constantly told them it was of no use, that the fish were scarcely ever taken, &c., went out on the lower studding-sail boom with a grains (a large strong fork of five barbed points) and a long line attached ; he had scarcely sat five minutes, when he struck and hauled up a fine boneto, to the exceeding great delight of the spectators, whose mania for the sport was tenfold increased by the seeming ease of the achievement. But it was a lucky accident that was not repeated by any one, and Mr. Meredith, being quite satisfied with having caught one, did not make another attempt.

It was a large handsome fish, very much the shape of a salmon, and presenting a succession of rich iridescent colours, such as are described in the dolphin when dying. It was cooked, and served, at least part of it, at our table ; but being fried, and rather dry and hard, it was not much admired.

I was extremely curious to see a real live dolphin, for my ideas of the creature were such a singular medley of classical-picture dolphins as big as calves, with fat tritons astride upon them ; and spouting-fountain dolphins, much of the same character, with heads bored like the rose of a watering-pot ; and public-house sign-board dolphins, something between St. George's dragon, and a legless, curly-tailed pig—that I wished to have my wavering notions somewhat settled : and one bright day in the tropics, as we lay becalmed or nearly so, I was leaning over the vessel's side, looking deep, deep into the bluest of all blue water, clear and bright as crystal, when three fish, of a kind quite new to me, came close to the ship, swimming to and fro, as if examining the state of our coppering; some one said very quietly, " Hush! those are dolphins," and so I guessed, but not from any resemblance they bore to my ancient friends of the name. These were really very beautiful; their size I cannot accurately tell, for I found myself so often deceived in the relative proportion of things seen in a similar manner. The boneto, as it swam past, only seemed to me the size of a large mackerel, and when brought on deck I found it exceeded that of a salmon. The dolphins might be four feet long, or more, of a slender shape, with a head rather blunt than pointed, but not in the least heavy or clumsy-looking : on the contrary, I never saw anything more elegant than their form and motion; their long bodies, as they swam, making a perfect " line of beauty " of several curves, and their large fins and tails waving like fans in the water.

Their colour appeared a delicate silvery blue, deepening by parts into purple; and as they partially turned up their bright sides to the sun, a gleam of prismatic colours gave evidence of there being at least some truth in the story of their rainbow hues when dying.

Much to my satisfaction, no attempt was made to capture any of these; I noticed them for some time sporting round the vessel, and then they passed on, having most permanently established my faith in the beauty of the dolphin and the ignorance of his carvers and limners.

CHAPTER III.

Calm in the Tropics—Sharks—Turtle—Ianthina—Shovel-board—" Crossing the Line "—Loss of the North Star—Southern Constellations—Moonlight in the Tropics—Sunsets—Waterspouts—" Sundogs."

A CALM at sea in the tropics, though by no means desirable for a continuance, is yet very beautiful for a short time; one may well endure a few hours' delay, even in such a climate, for the sake of observing the novel expression of the face of nature. The usually restless sea, the very emblem of life and vigour, seems in a deep slumber; not a ripple nor the tiniest wave that ever broke ruffles its glassy smoothness; it might now serve to typify death rather than life, but for a slow, long, heavy swell, that seems to lift up the drowsy waters as it rolls along; now and then the peculiar dorsal fin of a shark cuts through the still, sluggish mass, or a turtle, fast asleep, floats by, basking in the fervid sunshine.

On such a day as this, when every one felt particularly disposed to envy the fishes, and the life of a frog in a cool brook seemed the height of luxury, a boat was lowered, and a party of five, including Mr. Meredith, put off a considerable distance for the purpose of bathing, though the ostensible reason was " merely to see how the ship looked." I sat at work under the awning, looking from time to time at the boat, until it was so far away that the swell hid it from my view, and then heard those who could still see it from the shrouds say that the five were bathing, and some of them far away from the boat, among whom I very justly supposed was my husband, from his being an excellent swimmer.

The next instant one of the men aloft screamed out, " Oh God! there are two large sharks close to them !" *My* feelings *may* perhaps be imagined—certainly not expressed. The probability was that the swell would hide the monsters from their victims until too late for escape. *I* could see the sharks, which were on the top of a swell, but not the boat, which lay in the hollow beyond; and, almost wild with terror, joined my weak voice to the shouts of warning sent from the ship, till I heard the welcome cry, " They are all safe." The bathers had not seen the sharks till after they returned to the boat, when immediately the huge monsters rose alongside and followed for some distance, doubtless in the hope of another chance, in which, I scarcely need say, they were disappointed.

Several turtle were seen that day: the boating party nearly captured a large one, but it escaped; with a smaller one they were more adroit, finding it soundly

> " Sleeping on the water,
> And by good fortune, gliding softly, caught her,"

much to the satisfaction of the " gastronomes;" but either the cook or the turtle was deficient in good qualities, for it was greatly inferior to the same article as dressed on shore.

During the morning's excursion many of those beautiful and delicate shells the *Ianthina fragilis* were observed floating about. Mr. Meredith brought me two fine ones with the animal in, and I put them in a basin of sea-water to observe them. The head of the creature, instead of being close to the aperture of the shell, seemed some distance within, half a whorl at least, and the intervening space filled by a quantity of bubbly membrane, which likewise protruded from the aperture, of a deep violet colour; the shell was a lighter shade of the same lovely hue, and on removing the animal from it after death, my hands were so deeply stained with purple that it was some days before they lost the marks. The bubbles, which occupied the mouth of the shell, appeared only filled with air, and I supposed them to be employed by the creature as a float; most probably he has the power of discharging the air from them (in the same way that the nautilus is supposed to do, from the inner chambers of his shell) when he wishes to sink, although I did not observe any effort of the kind; but very possibly some of the delicate organs might have been injured, and their power destroyed, before the fragile things reached me.

Every one remembers the wise and cogent reason which worthy " Master Slender " assigns for his " not abiding the smell of roast meat," namely, that he once " broke his shins when playing at *shovel-board* with a master of fence for a dish of stewed prunes ;" but perhaps many, like myself, have been long in ignorance of the nature of this renowned game. One of our friends on board having proposed it as a good amusement in calm days, and when the ship was tolerably steady, it became very popular among the gentlemen, and proved a source of much diversion to me as a looker-on.

A square of about three feet diameter, divided into nine small squares, is chalked on the deck, forward, and a figure marked in each square, from 1 up to 9. The players have each two or three " boards," being circular pieces of inch-thick wood, about four inches wide; these are thrown slidingly along the deck, and of course aimed at the highest numbers ; if they are lucky enough to rest there, the next player endeavours to *shovel* them out, and leave his own in ; those counting most at the end winning the game. Any one standing in the way of a well-thrown shovel-board, and feeling the keenness of the blow, will fully commiserate poor Master Slender's mischance.

As we neared the " line," many grave discussions were held as to the degree of licence to be allowed the sailors in their usual commemorative sports on the occasion of crossing it ; and poor Neptune's humble and complimentary petition lay so long unanswered at head-quarters, that few or no preparations were made among the crew. Unfortunately the harmony and good feeling which uninterruptedly pervaded our own especial " coterie " was far from universal in the small community on board ; and any general participation in the mummery and somewhat rough usage of the sea-king's visit was therefore refused, the maskers being forbidden to come on the quarter-deck.

This being understood, the usual ceremony of Neptune's hailing the ship was effectively performed overnight, the god taking his departure in a fiery chariot, which matter-of-fact people will persist in explaining to be only a tar-barrel lighted and set afloat. The next day his Majesty, gorgeously attired in a painted canvas crown, and robes to correspond, with a magnificent display of oakum in the shape of hair and beard, accompanied by his secretary, chaplain, coachman, and other general officers of state similarly accoutred, approached the quarter-deck, on which we were all assembled, and made a very clever speech. Mr. Meredith, as spokesman of our party, replied with due form and etiquette, and begged to offer, as a token of our allegiance and duty, a tribute of certain monies, which his Majesty most graciously ordered his secretary to receive with all due acknowledgments. Mr. Meredith then ventured a supposition that his Majesty was fond of sporting, and expressed a hope that he was not much annoyed by poachers in his kingdom.—" Why, no, sir," replied the god, " not much; but *you* know, sir, there are *some* daring rascals who don't care whose fish they catch ;" and in the laugh that followed this attack on the captor of the boneto, his Majesty and suite, which included a nondescript dragon-like monster, with a very extensive canvas tail, whom Neptune termed his dog, turned towards their allotted scene of action ; and the uproar and riot that followed, caused by the determined resistance of the " intermediate" passengers to his godship's baptismal ceremonies of shaving and washing, soon drove me to my own cabin, where I remained till order was restored.

Our Neptune on the occasion was a fine tall fellow, usually known as " Long Bill," who had served some years in a man-of-war, and was a general favourite on board ; and being rather a genius in his way, would no doubt have " got up " the " masque" much more effectively, had he known it would be permitted.

We happened to cross the line on my birth-day, July 20th, so that I began my new year in a new hemisphere.

Among the many strange changes which a passage from one side of the world to the other has shown me, I do not know one thing that I *felt* so much as the loss of the North Star. Night after night I watched it, sinking lower—lower; and the well-known " Great Bear " that I had so gazed at even from a child, that it seemed like the face of an old friend, was fast going too ; it was like parting from my own loved home-faces over again. I thought of so many times and places associated in my mind with those bright stars; of those who had gazed on them beside me, some of whom had for ever passed from earth,—and of the rest, who might say that we should ever meet again? Those stars seemed a last link uniting us, but it was soon broken—they sunk beneath the horizon, and the new constellations of the southern hemisphere seemed to my partial eyes far less splendid.

The Magellanic clouds made me constantly wish for a view of
their starry hosts through a good astronomical telescope, as I believe they are among the "resolvable" nebulæ. The southern
portion of the galaxy, too, is very beautiful, tracing its double
path of glory over the heavens, and showing so much brighter
in the clear atmosphere of the tropics. The Southern Cross
scarcely satisfied my expectations : I hardly knew myself what
those were, but it seemed less clearly defined than the celestial
maps had represented it. I think many other groups of stars
form quite as perfect crosses. But the crowning glory of tropical nights is the moon. I remember an enthusiastic friend, on his
return from the shores of the Mediterranean, telling me I had
never seen *moonlight*—that there never was such a thing in
England ; and I now began to believe him. There is certainly
as much difference between moonlight in England and in the
tropics, as between twilight and sunshine. The full flood of
radiance that is shed on every object renders all as plainly visible
as in broad noon-day, but the soft colour of the light is delight-
fully refreshing to the eye wearied by the insupportable glare of
a tropical sun. It almost seemed as if we ought to follow the
moon's bright example, and "turn night into day," for it was by
far the pleasantest time to be awake.

Having an excellent common telescope, we enjoyed tracing
out the well-known map of the moon's disc, much more clearly
than I ever saw it before. The same glass enabled us to observe
well the belts and satellites of Jupiter, the moon-like form of
Venus, and, more indistinctly, Saturn and his ring. We frequently saw beautiful meteors and "shooting stars ;" and the
bright silent lightning, flashing in the horizon, beguiled many a
weary half-hour.

The sunsets too ! the indescribably glorious sunsets, so swiftly
changing, and so splendid in every change, were among my constant enjoyments. Pen and ink are vain to tell their wondrous
beauty ; nothing but the pencils of Turner or Danby, in their
most inspired moods, could give a shadow of it. I remember one
evening a most singular appearance ; a dense bank of dark clouds
had totally obscured the sun whilst yet high in the heavens, and
behind which he sunk, leaving, as a record of his past glory,
golden lines traced on the higher ridges of the thick vapoury screen.

CHAP. III.] WATERSPOUTS. 21

Some minutes afterwards a strange light gleamed redly forth; and on looking towards the sunset clouds, we saw, as through small windows in the dark wall, close to the water's edge, the sun's fiery eye, glaring along the sea in a track of molten flame. The effect was as strange as it was new to me; and we never after saw a similar appearance.

Frequently the sunset sky seemed a celestial "Field of the Cloth of Gold," with regal banners of purple streaming across it. At other times bright landscapes of fairy cloud-realms spread forth, where

"Hills above hills, and Alps on Alps arose,"

glowing in gem-like hues, as fleeting as they were fair. How often have I exclaimed, " *This* is the loveliest sunset we have had!" for all were so beautiful, the present one seemed ever the brightest.

We had comparatively few of the heavy falls of rain common in the tropics, but one day they visited us pretty liberally, in sudden squalls, between which the sun blazed out with double intensity. On that day several waterspouts appeared, traversing the sea with great velocity, but fortunately they only permitted us a distant view of their dangerous performances. One seemed to travel a considerable way in the wake of the ship, and we almost feared would overtake us. We could clearly see the column of whirling water, ending in a cloud above, and the churning foam at its base, as it rapidly advanced, but it apparently dispersed in a sudden squall that crossed its path.

Many of the appearances called by sailors "sun dogs" occurred during the showery weather. They exhibit the prismatic colours, and I used to think them portions of rainbows, which they exactly resemble, but are broad and short, and always rest on the water. A lunar rainbow was seen one evening, but it was fast fading before I observed it, and had then but little more colour than a halo.

It is curious to notice how much more we observe the aspects and objects of the sea and sky when our own especial element, the *earth*, is absent from our view; how much more desirous we feel to cultivate our acquaintance with the sun, moon, and stars; the clouds, rainbows, meteors; the ocean and its mighty mysteries, when thus severed from accustomed scenes, pursuits, and speculations.   In the monotony of all days at sea, any variation is an event ; a new fish seen swimming by, or an oddly shaped cloud, makes a white day in one's calendar ; and the remembrance of their comparative greatness at the time has perhaps caused me to invest with undue importance many trivial matters scarcely worth the recital.

CHAPTER IV.

Whales and "jets-d'eau" — Birds—Boatswain—Boobies—Cape Pigeon—
Mischief of Idleness—"Mr. Winkles" at Sea—Great Albatross—Nelly—
Stormy Petrel—Blue Petrel—Sailors' Delicacies—Stormy Weather.

VERY different from the doubtful notions I held about dolphins
were my ideas of a whale as seen at sea, for in the representation
of these huge monsters of the deep, all painters and gravers are
unanimous in opinion, and alike in their mode of portraiture. Accordingly I knew perfectly well, when summoned from my cabin
by the report of a whale being in sight, that I should behold an
enormous black mass standing far out of the water, with a huge
semicircular mouth surmounted by two trumpet-like apertures,
from which a double stream of clear water was perpetually flung
some forty or fifty feet into the air, falling again in a graceful
curve, precisely like the "jets-d'eau" in ancient gardens. With
such a foregone conclusion as to what was to be seen, I came on
deck, and gazed round in search of the living fountain I describe ;
my inability to discover it being rendered tenfold more vexatious
by hearing the sailors and others exclaim, "There she spouts !"
"She spouts again !" till Mr. Meredith, seeing me vacantly scanning the whole horizon, drew my attention to one particular
spot, where, after looking intently for about a minute, I observed
something like a puff of steam rise gently from the water ; and
this was the *spouting* of a whale ! Many a time since have I
laughed at the recollection, but the shock my faith then received
it will never recover, nor shall I ever forget the useful lesson
I then learned, not to take too much on credit.

This absurd habit which people have got into, of depicting the
whale as spouting distinct streams of water to such a height,
though it may have originated in ignorance, cannot in these
days of universal knowledge be permitted that apology for its
continuance. But having once created so charming a fiction, I
imagine these good folks are loth to rob the poor whales of the

childish admiration our school-book pictures receive, and so doubtless they will spout steeple high till the whole real race is extinct—a palpable proof of the triumph of romance over reality. The spout-holes are simply the nostrils of the animal, and when, as he swims along, these chance to be below the surface of the water at the moment he breathes, the act of respiration blows the water from within and above the nostrils into the air in the form of vapour or steam.

The only time when anything like a stream proceeds from the blow-holes is when the creature is severely wounded; then he sometimes spouts blood. Frequently a thin haze is observed by whalers blowing along the sea, like the foamy crest of a wave scudding before the wind; and following back the course of this with the eye, the " blow " of a whale is often observed, sending off these whiffs of vapour. If seen between the boats and the shore, an inexperienced person would often mistake it for smoke on land.

A parasitical polype, peculiar to the whale, is generally found firmly attached to the skin of the animal when full-grown, especially about the head and lips; but it is a curious fact, and one which I do not remember ever to have seen noticed, that at the time of birth (and even previously) the young whales are marked with exact impressions or scars, of the precise form of the polypes, in those parts where afterwards the real parasites invariably appear.

We had hitherto seen very few birds; one day a beautiful white one, with two very long tail-feathers, flew over and round the ship, and many murderous proposals were made by the idlers to shoot it; but my entreaties for its life, strengthened by the superstitious warnings of the sailors, who seemed to regard it as a good omen of something or other, preserved the poor thing, and I had the happiness of seeing it fly away unharmed. It was the boatswain, or frigate-bird. We only saw that one bird of the kind during the passage, and certainly it was the most beautiful as well as the rarest of our feathered visitants.

Soon afterwards two or three boobies paid us a flying call, very possibly to see some relatives on board; of course the ties of affinity preserved them from molestation. Lord Byron, in his inimitable description of Juan's shipwreck, very aptly associates

the *noddy* with the boobies, but no noddy accompanied ours, that
I am aware of.

We fell in with numbers more of the feathered people, as we
increased our distance from the equator; most abundant were
the Cape pigeons, or " passenger's friend" (*Procellaria Capen-
sis*). Had the *sobriquet* been " passenger's *victim*," it had been
far more appropriate, for it appears the universal custom—shame
on those who make it so!—to massacre these poor harmless and
really beautiful birds for the mere wanton love of destruction.
Every one possessed of a gun, powder, and shot aids in the
slaughter, or at least does his worst; and besides the killed, I
have watched many and many a poor wounded bird, disabled
from flying or procuring food, float helplessly away to perish in
pain and starvation, because some heartless blockhead had no other
resource to kill time than breaking its leg or wing. Often did I
think of the line in the good old nursery hymn,

> " For Satan finds some mischief still
> For idle hands to do;"

and never was its truth more fully exemplified.

Hooks, baited with pork, were also used to *fish* for them; but
as very few were caught in this manner, it proved a far more
harmless amusement, and the exhibition of their natural voracity,
which it occasioned, somewhat dulled one's sympathy with them.
The moment a freshly-baited hook was flung astern, a crowd of
pigeons would assemble round it, flying, swimming, scuffling
through the water, as the tempting morsel skipped along the surface, scolding and driving each other away with most expressive
cries. Very probably a great albatross is watching the result, as
he hovers with a still, solemn aspect above the bustling, squabbling
crowd. The pigeons succeed in pulling the pork from the hook,
and the tumult is redoubled when, in the heat of the battle, the
booty is dropped, and the wary albatross, with a sudden and sure
plunge, relieves them from all further contention by appropriat-
ing the dainty morsel to his own use. Such a scene is acted
twenty times a day; sometimes the bird greedily swallows the
bait and hook together, and flies high into the air, whence the
fisher gradually winds him down; but this is no warning to the
survivors, who are as eager for the next throw of the treacherous
bait as if none of their number had suffered by its deception.

The Cape pigeon is a small kind of albatross, much larger in the body than a pigeon, and with a great span of wing for its size. The plumage is white, beautifully marked with black on the back and wings, and their black eyes have a very peculiar, but soft and pleasing expression. The various attitudes of a group of these pretty birds, as they are seen closely following the ship—some swimming, others sitting on the water, or running along it with outspread wings, or just lighting down—are really very graceful and beautiful, and were a constant source of amusement to me, whenever their valorous enemies allowed them a truce.

A sportsman of the "Winkles" school is quite dangerous enough on shore, but when to all the awkwardness of such characters is added their utter helplessness at sea, and their invariable rule of stumbling along, with a loaded gun on full cock aimed directly at the nearest person's head, it may easily be conceived what perilous chances occur. Of this class were several violent specimens on board our vessel, all most determined, but most innocent foes of the unfortunate pigeons, as it most frequently happened that they hit a rope or a sail, instead of the bird, having no idea of allowing for the motion of the vessel. The appearance of these gentry on the quarter-deck, weapon in hand, soon became my signal of retreat.

The Cape pigeons are very rarely met with beyond their peculiar track, which extends from 35° to 55° south latitude, within which boundaries they encircle the globe as with a living zone.

The great white albatross (*Diomedia exulans*) fully realized all my ideas of its grandeur and solemnity. I never saw it without thinking of Coleridge's wild and wondrous tale of the "Ancient Mariner;" nor can there possibly be any creature more fitted to take part in such a dread and ghostly narrative than this melancholy, grave, and most majestic bird. It soars along with widely-expanded wings that often measure fifteen or eighteen feet between the tips, with an even, solemn flight, rarely seeming to stir, but as if merely floating along. Now and then a slow flapping motion serves to raise him higher in the air, but the swift movement and busy flutter of other birds seem beneath his dignity. He sails almost close to you, like a silent spectre. Nothing of life appears in his still, motionless form, but his keen piercing eye, except that occasionally his head turns slightly, and betrays a sharp, prying expression, that somewhat shakes your belief in the lordly indifference he would fain assume ; and if you fling overboard a piece of rusty pork, the disenchantment is complete, and you see that long curiously-crooked beak exercising its enormous strength in an employment so spectral a personage could scarcely be suspected of indulging. There is another kind of albatross, nearly as large as the " great" one, with a small portion of black on its wings, that appears exactly similar in habits to its more renowned relative ; but these pied ones are more numerous.

Another kind, that the sailors called " Nelly" (*Diomedia fuliginosa?*), of a dusky, smoky hue, was very abundant, and, I am sorry to say, very frequently destroyed, although, by the great thickness of the plumage or some other protecting cause, their lives were often most strangely preserved. After falling plump into the water, to all appearance shot *dead*, many would float away a short distance, and then, turning over to their proper position, perting up the head, and giving their wings an experimental flutter, as if to ascertain that no damage was done, away they flew unharmed, greatly to my delight and the confusion of their enemies. These surprising resuscitations gained for them with us the name of " immortals."

All the various species of albatross have the same kind of expressive eye I mentioned in describing the Cape pigeon ; a gentle, yet withal shrewd glance, and in some a few darker feathers round the eye, add to the soft expression, just as long dark eyelashes do in a human face.

What the flying-fish is, compared with the porpoise, such is the light, swift little petrel beside the slow, solemn albatross. Glancing, dipping, skimming about, or running along the water with half-spread wings, they are all life and activity :

" Up and down, up and down,
" From the base of the waves to the billow's crown ;"

they appear mere happy little birds ; whilst those awful, funereal creatures give one the idea of unhappy disembodied spirits, condemned to sail about these inhospitable seas till their penance is done.

There are two species of petrel in the vicinity of the Cape : one,

the common kind, is nearly black, and, I believe, is the same
which frequents the northern British islands; the other, far more
beautiful, is a very delicate blue, and more slight in form than
the dark one. The two kinds keep in separate flocks, and I
could only obtain a good view of the blue ones with a glass, as
they are very shy, and never ventured near the ship—a very wise
precaution.

Nothing comes amiss to sailors in the way of eatables; nor,
when we consider the wretched fare on which they usually sub-
sist in merchant vessels, can their ready adoption of anything
that promises a variety create surprise. The rank, oily, dis-
gustingly high-scented sea-birds that were caught by the passengers, were all begged and eaten by the crew. One day a very
large gull or albatross was handed over to them, and duly
demolished; and on some one's inquiring how it tasted, a steerage
passenger very gravely declared it to be " very like partridge !"
When the bird came on deck, quantities of pure oil poured from
its beak,—and then to hear of its eating " *like partridge !*"

Very soon after passing the Cape, wet, cold, stormy weather set
in, and banished me from my accustomed place on deck to my
cabin, where, with dead-lights securely stopping the stern-windows and the skylight closely shut, I slept away as much of the
weary day as I could, and sat shivering in cloaks and furs the
remainder, for there was not a stove on board. That *was* a
weary time; tremendous gales blowing, seas being constantly
shipped, and streaming into the mess-cabin, though rarely into
ours; the galley-fire continually being put out; and, worst of all,
the ship rolling and pitching so violently that one would think
each plunge must be her last. Often in the night, when the
roaring din around drove away all chance of sleep, I have had a
light struck to lie awake by, the darkness seemed so terrible amid
those horrid noises. The howling and screaming of the wind,
the roaring and dashing water sounding close in one's ears, and
every part of the vessel complaining, in its own particular tone
of creaking, cracking, or groaning, made up such a frightful
uproar, that it seemed sometimes as if a whole legion of fiends
were aboard.

Frequent terrific crashes among the crockery and glass ware
produced crashes of words, not " writ in choice Italian," but

spoken in a rough and wrathful tone, from captain and steward; the result being a sad diminution of cups and wine-glasses. Such was our dilapidated condition, that two or three old powder-canisters and preserve-jars formed the entire drinking equipage of the cabin table, when the last wine-glass, long the innocent cause of direst jealousy, was lamentably broken. Being rich in the possession of two small white respectable-looking marmalade jars, we took especial care of our valuable "breakfast service," and, until one of our treasures went to pieces in a squall, were the envy of our less fortunate fellow-voyagers; but this general poverty in conveniences was productive of so much merriment, that I doubt if the finest services of china and cut-glass would have served half as well to while away the slowly passing time. A little wit, as of any other good thing, must go a great way at sea, where any change of the too-often grumbling tone of conversation is acceptable.

It is very common for people to talk and write of waves running "*mountains* high," but I confess I always used to make a very liberal allowance for exaggeration and imagery in these cases; and I well remember once joining in the laugh of incredulity, when a gentleman told myself and other young people that he had seen waves of which two would fill the breadth of the Menai Strait, where we then were. I had not then been a long voyage myself; I had not looked and trembled at the scene I witnessed one Sunday morning after a two days' gale, during which I had remained below. The wind had abated considerably, but we could only carry a close-reefed mainsail, and were "scudding" along. Any attempt to describe the vast, awful grandeur of the scene seems absurd—it is so impossible for anything but the eye itself to represent it to the mind; I feel dizzy with the mere remembrance.

When I came on deck, the ship lay as in an immense valley of waters, with huge waves, *mountain* waves, indeed (one of which would have flooded both shores of the Menai), circling us all around: then slowly we seemed to climb the ascent, and, poised on the summit of the rolling height, could look along the dark and dreary waste of ocean heaving with giant billows far and wide; then, plunging down into the next frightful abyss, the labouring vessel seemed doomed;—I fancied already the rush of water in my ears, when, with a violent pitch and shudder, the ship bounded along again, over another mountain, and down another valley, in long and slow succession again and again, till I grew accustomed to the scene, and could gaze without thinking I looked upon our vast and miserable grave.

There were the ghost-like albatrosses sailing solemnly above the tops of the towering billows, or diving beside us into the yawning gulf,—sailing about with the same unruffled plumes, the same quiet, wary eye, and majestic demeanour, that they wore in the brightest calm. Who could doubt their supernatural attributes? Certainly not a spirit-chilled landswoman, with Coleridge's magic legend perpetually repeating itself to her. I wish some of its good and beautiful lines were as familiar and impressive in the minds and thoughts of others as they are in mine:—

> " Farewell, farewell—but this I tell
> To thee, thou wedding guest !
> *He prayeth well, who loveth well*
> Both man and bird and beast.
>
> He prayeth best, who loveth best
> All things, both great and small ;
> For the dear God, who loveth us,
> He made and loveth all."

CHAPTER V.

A VIEW of the little volcanic island of St. Paul's was the only thing that served to vary the tedium of our stormy passage across the Indian Ocean ; and our view being rather a distant one, the only benefit we derived from it was the introduction of a new topic of conversation.—I believe excellent fish are very abundant there ; and, as the story goes, you may stand and pull your dinner out of the cold salt-water with one hand, and drop it into a hot fresh spring to cook with the other ! I know not if the renowned Baron Munchausen ever visited St. Paul's, but this savours something of his quality. A few wild pigs are there now likewise ; but the island is a mere volcanic rock, or rather the crater of an extinct volcano, with no trees or bushes, and but very scanty vegetation of any kind. The hot springs show that volcanic agency is still busy there.

Violent gales, cold and rainy weather, were long our portion, but a favourable change occurred in time to decide our route to be through Bass's Straits, which would not have been prudent in the more boisterous weather ; and the longer passage round Van Diemen's Land seemed an intolerable prolongation of our most irksome captivity.

Never shall I forget the feeling of intense pleasure with which I greeted the sight of land again, as we passed among the numerous islands in the Straits. Bare, barren as they were, I thought them lovely as the Elysian fields, for they were *land*, solid, firm, dry land. How we leaned over the vessel's side, *smelling* the shore !—enjoying the fine earthy, fragrant smell that our sea-seasoned noses were so quick to detect in every puff of wind that

came over the islands. We passed several very singular rocks*
early in the morning of this most happy day, and went sailing
on, with a fair breeze, a bright sunny blue sky, and an ever-
changing, ever-new prospect around. We passed so near the
islands of " Kent's Group," and another called the " Judgment,"
as to discern flocks of seal sleeping on the rocks; thousands of
sea-birds, named by sailors " mutton-birds," were flying or floating around us, and often diving for a considerable distance; and,
most beautiful of all in this bright picture, numerous vessels
were in sight, all bound for the same port as ourselves; and after
each traversing a different path, were here, as it were, falling
into the common high road for the Australian metropolis.

Those " mutton-birds" I have just mentioned form a most
curious and interesting community. I know not if their habits
have been observed by naturalists, being myself totally out of
the reach of books of reference on all similar subjects; but the
particulars I have heard from my husband, whose early wanderings familiarised him with many of the native creatures of the
Australian islands, struck me as being very curious. The
birds are about the size of a wild-duck, with handsome black
plumage, shot with metallic shades of green or brown, accordingly as the light falls on it; they are web-footed, and the beak
is similar in form to that of the albatross family. They live
wholly at sea the chief part of the year, but on one particular
day in spring—November 1st, never varying many hours in the
time—they come in from sea in countless myriads, filling the
air with clouds of their dark wings as they hurry ashore on some
of the islands in Bass's Straits, where their " rookeries," as the
sealers term them, are made. These are burrows in the earth,
covering many of the islands; and the first care of the birds on
returning is to scratch them out clean from any rubbish that
has accumulated, and put them in order for habitation, and often
to make new ones. This preparatory business occupies about a
fortnight, and then the swarming squadrons put to sea again for
another fortnight or three weeks, not a bird remaining behind.
At the end of this time they return in a body as before, and with
much noise and bustle take up their abode in the rookeries, and

---

* Called, I *think*, the Judge and Clerks.

there lay their eggs and sit. The parent birds share between them the " domestic duties," taking it in turns to remain on the nest or go out to seek their food, which chiefly consists of a green slimy matter like sea-weed. They remain on shore until the young ones are a third part grown, and immensely fat, like masses of blubber, when the old birds leave them and go off to sea. The young ones, unable to leave the rookeries, are sustained meanwhile by their own fat ; and by the time that is tolerably reduced, their wings are grown strong enough for flight, and they also quit the rookery and go to sea.

The men employed in sealing on these islands derive their chief sustenance from the mutton-birds, which they take in various ways. One very successful method of snaring them is thus practised : — A high pen of stakes wattled together is made on a low part of the coast, into which the poor mutton-birds, who always run down to the water to take wing, are driven with dogs and shouting, and there, as they cannot rise off the land, they can be killed at leisure. An extensive trade in their feathers is also carried on, but these have generally a strong and unpleasant smell ; so that a " mutton-bird pillow" is spoken of as something proverbially disagreeable. Great quantities of the birds are cured by the sealers for sale, and I am told that their flavour is similar to that of a red-herring.

Very early on the morning of September 27th, Mr. Meredith was requested to go on deck and identify the land we were then passing, cloudy weather for two days having prevented any observation being taken, and our exact whereabouts being therefore doubtful. The unknown cliffs were immediately pronounced to be the headlands of Botany Bay !—Our weary wayfaring was nearly done, the next break in the iron-bound coast that rose dark and threateningly before us would be our welcome haven, Sydney Cove !

In an absolute whirl of delight and excitement, with bright looks and quick eager voices all around, I hastened to put up a few packages ready to take ashore, continually interrupting myself to go on deck and mark our progress. The agitation on board was universal, and the transformations little short of miraculous ; passenger-chrysalids were turning into butterflies every instant. Gentlemen, whose whole outer vestments for the past

D

month would have scarcely brought half-a-crown in Rag-Fair,
suddenly emerged from their cabins exquisites of the first water ;
and ladies, whose bronzed and scorched straw-bonnets would have
been discarded long before by a match-girl, now appeared in
delicate silks or satins of the latest London fashion. Gala dresses
and holiday faces were the order of the day ; perhaps a child
going home from school may feel as happy as I did, but the
degree of delight could scarcely be excelled.

The entrance to Port Jackson is grand in the extreme. The
high, dark cliffs we had been coasting along all morning, suddenly
terminate in an abrupt precipice, called the South Head, on
which stand the lighthouse and signal-station. The North Head
is a similar cliff, a bare bluff promontory of dark horizontal
rocks ; and between these grand stupendous pillars, as through a
colossal gate, we entered Port Jackson.

The countless bays and inlets of this noble estuary render it
extremely beautiful ; every minute, as we sailed on, a fresh vista
opened on the view, each, as it seemed, more lovely than the
last ; the pretty shrubs, growing thickly amid the rocks, and down
to the water's edge, added infinitely to the effect, especially as
they were really green, a thing I had not dared to expect ; but it
was spring, and everything looked fresh and verdant.

Here and there, on some fine lawny promontory or rocky
mount, white villas and handsome cottages appeared, encircled
with gardens and shrubberies, looking like the pretty "cottages
ornées" near some fashionable English watering-place ; and
perched amid as picturesque, but less cultivated scenery, were the
cottages of pilots, fishermen, &c., making, to my ocean-wearied
eyes, an Arcadia of beauty. Near the North Head is the
quarantine-ground, off which one unlucky vessel was moored
when we passed ; and on the brow of the cliff a few tombstones
indicate the burial-place of those unhappy exiles who die
during the time of ordeal, and whose golden dreams of the far-
sought land of promise lead but to a lone and desolate grave on
its storm-beaten shore.

We very narrowly escaped a serious accident even in the
port. A large vessel was moored in mid-channel, and our
pilot could not decide on which side he would pass her, until
we were so near that a collision seemed inevitable, but we for-

tunately cleared her, with not two feet to spare, and pursued our course.

During a light shower which fell shortly after, amid the bright sunshine, a most beautiful rainbow appeared, seeming like a smile of welcome to my new country. It spanned over one of the many lovely little bays, and was very broad, so that, although the centre had a considerable elevation, it wholly rested on the water, which, with the rocks, trees, and hills beyond, and the snow-white sands of the bay, shone in all the graduated shades of the bright prismatic colours. It was beautiful beyond description.

The pure white silvery sand which forms the beach in several of these picturesque coves, gives them a peculiarly bright appearance; it is much valued, I believe, by glass-makers at home, and often taken as ship's ballast, for that purpose.

As we neared Sydney, several rocky islets appeared, some rising like ruined forts and castles, and richly adorned with verdant shrubs down to the edge of the bright, clear, deep blue water, that reflected them so perfectly, one could scarcely tell where substance and shadow joined. One of them is named Shark Island; another larger one, Garden Island; and a little one, bearing the unmeaning and not very refined name of " Pinchgut," is now the site of a small fort or battery.

The remarkable clearness of the atmosphere particularly struck me, in looking at distant houses or other objects, everything, however remote, seeming to have such a *clean*, distinct outline, so different to the diffused effect of an English landscape; not that I should like it in a *picture* so well as our softer and more rounded perspective, but in a new place, where one likes to see everything plainly, it is very pleasant. The bright white villas seemed almost to cut into their surrounding trees, so sharp the corners appeared; and the universal adjunct of a veranda or piazza in front, served to remind us that we were in a more sunny clime than dear, dull Old England, where such permanent sun-shades would be as intolerable as they are here necessary.

The harbour-master's boat was soon alongside, and he, with the physician, came on board, to perform their respective duties of inquiry and examination, and to hear the last news from *home*. No vessel had arrived from thence for a month, an unusually long interval, and intelligence was anxiously expected;

D 2

but during the day of our arrival and the following one, above a dozen English vessels poured in.

The pilot had informed us that wheat was at an enormous price in Sydney then, but his statement was not credited ; it was, however, only too correct, *twenty-seven shillings per bushel* being the average price, in consequence of the severe droughts, which had for two successive seasons destroyed the crops.

The crew of the harbour-master's boat were New Zealanders, fine intelligent-looking, copper-coloured fellows, clad in an odd composite style, their national dress and some British articles of apparel being blended somewhat grotesquely. The New Zealanders are much the noblest specimens of " savages " that I have ever met with. During our residence in Sydney I saw a chief walking along one of the principal streets, with his wife following him. I had often heard of and seen what is called majestic demeanour, but this untutored being, with his tattooed face and arms, and long shaggy mantle, fairly outdid even my imaginings of the majestic, as he paced deliberately along, planting his foot at every step as if he had an emperor's neck beneath it, and gazing with most royal indifference around him. There was the concentrated grandeur of a hundred regal mantles of velvet, gold, and ermine in the very sway of his flax-fringed cloak ; I never beheld anything so truly stately. I cannot say so much for his lady, a black-haired, brown-faced body, in a gaudy cotton-print gown, and (so far as I could judge) nothing else. She trotted after her lordly better-half, staring with unsophisticated curiosity at everything, apparently quite a novice in the busy scene ; but I verily believe, had you placed the man amidst the coronation splendours of Westminster Abbey, that he would not have been so " vulgar " as to betray surprise. Nor is their courtesy of manner in any degree inferior to their magnificent demeanour. I have heard my husband say, that when at New Zealand, he was treated by the chiefs with such kind, anxious hospitality, and true gentlemanly bearing, as might put to shame many an educated but less civilized European.

About noon we cast anchor opposite Fort Macquarie, a neat stone building, with a few cannon planted around it. Close alongside of us lay a Scotch emigrant ship, her deck thronged with crowds of both sexes and all ages, enlivened by the fearful din of some half-dozen bagpipers, who were all puffing, squeezing, and elbowing away with incomparable energy and perseverance, though, as they all seemed to be playing different airs, the melody produced was rather of a complex character.

Behind, or rather to the right of Fort Macquarie, was Government House, a long low building with a spacious veranda, in which sentinels were pacing to and fro; before it lay a fine green lawn, sloping towards, though not to, the water's edge, (quays intervening,) and around it grew noble trees, both European and Colonial, the English oak in its early spring garb of yellow green being here and there overtopped by the grand and more sombre Norfolk Island pine. A few other good houses were in view, but the chief of the town, or, as it must now be called, city, is built on the sides and at the head of a cove running at right angles with the stream in which we lay, which prevented the best parts from being observed, and the main portion of what was visible had an air of " Wapping" about it, by no means engaging.

The opposite or north shore of Port Jackson, here about two miles across, is of rather a monotonous character. Hills of no great elevation and very tame outline rise from the beach, dotted here and there with villas and cottages, their adjoining gardens making a pleasant green contrast with the uniform brown hue of the scrub. Numberless boats were pulling and sailing about, giving animation to the scene, and several of the vessels we had passed in Bass's Straits were working up the port; the life and bustle all around making a delightful change after our long solitary voyage; and when the boat came to take us ashore, my joy was complete. Once more seated in the slung chair, wrapped in the British flag, I gladly bade adieu to the good ship that had so long seemed to me a weary "prison-house," and soon, with-a delight that must be felt to be understood, stepped again on *land*.

And how happy a time it is—the first few days on shore after such a voyage! Every action of life is an enjoyment. I could walk, without the floor jumping about and pitching me over; could use *both* hands to brush my hair, instead of keeping one to hold on by; could absolutely set my wine-glass on the table without fear of its upsetting into my plate, though, by the bye,

I often caught myself carefully propping it up against something,
or looking above for the swing-tray to put it out of danger.
Then the abundant supply of water for ablutionary purposes is a
priceless luxury when first enjoyed after the limited allowance on
board ship ; and I often made the chambermaid smile by asking
if she could *spare* me another ewer-full. It is *fresh, clean* water
too, not flavoured either by a vinegar or rum cask, and can be
used without being " left to settle ! " Perhaps few ship-stewards
are *very* clean, but all are not *extremely* dirty, and therefore our
exquisite enjoyment of clean cups, glasses, plates, and forks, may
not be imagined by the generality of voyagers. Vegetables too,
after a long diet of pork and rice, were most acceptable. Fruit
was not in season, except loquats, a pleasant acid berry, the size
and shape of a gooseberry, with large kernel-like pippins. The
tree is a very handsome one, bearing large long leaves, and drooping clusters of white, deliciously fragrant blossoms, which are succeeded by the golden-coloured fruit.

When we remember that Sydney has risen within little more
than fifty years from the first settlement of the colony, its size,
appearance, and population are truly wonderful. It is a large
busy town, reminding me of portions of Liverpool or Bristol,
with many good buildings, though few have any pretension to
architectural beauty. The newer portions of the town are laid
out with regularity and advantage. One long street traverses its
whole length, about a mile and a half, full of good shops exhibiting
every variety of merchandise ; and in the afternoon, when the
ladies of the place drive out, whole strings of carriages may be
seen rolling about or waiting near the more " fashionable empo-
riums," that being the term in which Australian shopkeepers
especially delight. The vehicles are sometimes motley enough
in their equipment. Here and there appears a real London-built
chariot, brilliant in paint and varnish, and complete in every
luxury ; with a coachman, attired something like worthy Sam
Weller, " as a compo of footman, gardener, and groom," sitting
on a box innocent of hammercloth, and driving a pair of mean-
looking, under-sized horses terribly out of proportion with the
handsome, aristocratic-looking carriage behind them. Sometimes, but very rarely, you see a consistent, well-appointed equipage ; I think the tandem is more frequently turned out in good

style than any other kind: and as no "lady" in Sydney (your
grocers' and butchers' wives included) believes in the possibility
of walking, the various machines upon wheels, of all descriptions,
are very numerous; from the close carriage and showy barouche
or britzka, to the more humble four-wheeled chaise and useful
gig. Few ladies venture to risk their complexions to the exposure of an equestrian costume, and accordingly few appear on
horseback.

George Street seems to be by common consent considered as
the Pall-Mall, or rather as the "Park" of Sydney, and up and
down its hot, dusty, glaring, weary length go the fair wives and
daughters of the "citizens," enjoying their daily airing; whilst
close to the town is the beautiful Domain, a most picturesque
rocky promontory, thickly wooded and laid out in fine smooth
drives and walks, all commanding most exquisite views of Sydney
and its environs, the opposite shore, and the untiring ever-beau-
tiful estuary of Port Jackson. It was our favourite spot; even
after driving elsewhere out of town (for alas! the splendour of
George Street had no charms for me) we generally made one
circuit round the Domain, and as generally found ourselves the
only visitors. It was unfashionable, in fact, not the proper
thing at all, either to walk or drive in the Domain. It was a
notorious fact, that maid-servants and their sweethearts resorted
thither on Sundays, and of course that shocking circumstance
ruined its character as a place for their mistresses to visit; the
public streets being so much more select.

Lady Macquarie had this Domain laid out after her own plans;
walks and drives were cut through the rocks and shrubs, but no
other trees destroyed; seats placed at intervals, and lodges built
at the entrances. On the high point of the promontory some
large horizontal rocks have been slightly assisted by art into
the form of a great seat or throne, called Lady Macquarie's
Chair, above which an inscription informs the visitor to whose
excellent taste and benevolent feeling he is indebted for the improvement of this lovely spot. It always reminded me of Pierce-
field in Monmouthshire, but is far more beautiful, inasmuch as,
instead of the black-banked Wye, here the bright blue waves of
the bay wash the lower crags, and in place of looking only at
one opposite bank, here is a noble estuary with countless bays

and inlets, pretty villas and cottages, and dainty little islands, all bright and clear and sunny, with a cloudless sky above them. The trees are chiefly different species of Eucalyptus, or " gum-tree," some of which bear large and handsome flowers, having a remarkably sweet and luscious scent, like honey, with which they abound. The name Eucalyptus is admirably descriptive of the flower, meaning covered well with a lid; and each closed blossom is shaped like a goblet, with a pyramidal cover, which in due time falls, or is thrust off, by the crowd of squeezed-up stamens within, that quickly expand into a starry circle when released from their verdant prison. The leaves are mostly of a dull green, with a dry sapless look about them, more like old specimens in a herbarium than fresh living and growing things, and, being but thinly scattered on the branches, have a meagre appearance. They are, however, "evergreens," and in their peculiarity of habit strongly remind the observer that he is at the antipodes of England, or very near it, where everything seems topsy-turvy, for instead of the "fall of the leaf," here we have the stripping of the bark, which peels off at certain seasons in long pendent ragged ribands, leaving the disrobed tree almost as white and smooth as the paper I am now writing on. At first I did not like this at all, but now the clean stems of a young handsome gum-tree seem a pleasing variety amidst the sombre hues of an Australian forest.

Several species of tea-tree (Leptospermum) form the chief portion of the shrubbery here, producing their small pretty blossoms very abundantly, whilst various other shrubs and many species of acacia (generally called Mimosa or Wattle here) display innumerable novelties of leaf and flower to the admiring eyes of an English visitor. One beautiful shrub grows on some of the low rocks, which I have not observed elsewhere: the leaves are large, and not unlike those of a Camellia; the flower, in form, size, and colour, resembles a fine single yellow rose.

Opposite the south shore of the Domain, and forming the other boundary of a beautiful cove, is another similar point or promontory, called still by the native name of Wooloomooloo (the accent being on the first and last syllables), on which a number of elegant villas have been erected by the more wealthy residents in Sydney, being to that place what the Regent's Park

is to London. The views from many of these are beautiful in
the extreme, looking down into two bays, one on either side, and
beyond these to the town and port, with the magnificent heads
of the harbour closing the seaward prospect. Vines flourish
here luxuriantly, and many tropical plants and trees mingle with
those of European growth. Hedges are often formed of geraniums, and sometimes of the fruit-bearing cactus, called the
prickly pear (*C. opuntia*, or *C. nana?*), a detestable thing,
which if touched, even with strong leathern gloves, so penetrates
them with its fine long spines, that the hands of the unlucky
meddler are most annoyingly hurt by them. Some of our rarest
greenhouse passion-flowers grow here unsheltered, and flower profusely; and the Brugmansia often forms the centre of a grass
plot, with its graceful tent-like white bells hanging on it in hundreds. Geraniums thrive and grow very rapidly, but I did not
see any good ones; none that I should have thought worth cul-
tivating in England. A Horticultural Society has now been
established some years, and will doubtless be the means of
much improvement.

The Government Gardens are tastefully laid out round the
sloping head of a small bay between the Domain and Government House, and contain (besides abundant vineries, and all
other productive matters) a strange and beautiful assemblage of
dwellers in all lands, from the tall bamboo of India to the lowly
English violet. A group of graceful weeping-willows overhang
a pretty shady pool, where a statue, by an English sculptor
(Westmacott, I think), is now erected to General Bourke, formerly governor of New South Wales. It had not arrived when
we left Sydney, or I should have much rejoiced to see the first
specimen of high art which the colony has obtained, placed in so
lovely and, with us, so favourite a spot. The grand Norfolk
Island pine, the fig, orange, mulberry, and countless trees,
shrubs, and flowers new to me, add to the gay beauty of these
gardens; and when tired of roaming about the sunny and fragrant walks, there are grassy lawns and shaded seats—and such
a lovely prospect around, that, much as I should dislike to dwell
in Sydney, I left its beautiful gardens with great regret. Yet,
will it be believed, that even these are very little frequented by
the inhabitants? They are evidently, from some cause unknown

to me (but doubtless nearly allied to the cause of the Domain's desertion), not considered correctly fashionable by the fancied " exclusives " of the place, though constantly frequented by all new-comers; at all events, the former prefer the hot, glaring, dusty pavement of a town street for their promenade, to these delicious gardens.*

* Since writing the above, I have seen some remarks in a Sydney newspaper which imply a more general resort to the " Domain " than was the case at the time of which I speak. I rejoice to find that the beauties of so delightful a spot are becoming more properly estimated.

CHAPTER VI.

Sydney Market—Fish, &c.—Dust; Flies—Mosquitoes—Drive to the Light-
house—Flowers—Parrots—Black Cockatoos—Hyde Park—Churches—
Libraries—" Currency" population—Houses—Balls, &c.—Inns—Colonial
Newspapers.

THE market in Sydney is well supplied, and is held in a large
commodious building, superior to most provincial market-houses
at home. The display of fruit in the grape season is very
beautiful. Peaches also are most abundant, and very cheap ; apples
very dear, being chiefly imported from Van Diemen's Land,
and frequently selling at sixpence each. The smaller English
fruits, such as strawberries, &c., only succeed in a few situations
in the colony, and are far from plentiful. Cucumbers and all
descriptions of melon abound. The large green water-melon,
rose-coloured within, is a very favourite fruit, but I thought it
insipid. One approved method of eating it is, after cutting a
sufficiently large hole, to pour in a bottle of Madeira or sherry,
and mix it with the cold watery pulp. These melons grow to
an enormous size (an ordinary one is from twelve to eighteen
inches in diameter), and may be seen piled up like huge cannon-
balls at all the fruit-shop doors, being universally admired in this
hot, thirsty climate.

There are some excellent fish to be procured here, but I know
them only by the common Colonial names, which are frequently
misnomers. The snapper, or schnapper, is the largest with which
I am acquainted, and is very nice, though not esteemed a proper
dish for a dinner-party—why, I am at a loss to guess ; but I never
saw any native fish at a Sydney dinner-table—the preserved or
cured cod and salmon from England being served instead, at a
considerable expense, and, to my taste, it is not comparable with
the cheap fresh fish, but being expensive, it has become " fashionable," and that circumstance reconciles all things. The guard-
fish is long and narrow, about the size of a herring, with a very

singular head, the mouth opening at the top, as it were, and the lower jaw, or nose, projecting two-thirds of an inch beyond it. I imagine it must live chiefly at the bottom, and this formation enables it more readily to seize the food above it. They are most delicate little fish. The bream, a handsome fish, not unlike a perch in shape (but much larger, often weighing four or five pounds), and the mullet, but especially the latter, are excellent. The whiting, much larger than its English namesake, is perhaps the best of all; but I pretend to no great judgment as a gastronome. I thought the rock-oysters particularly nice, and they are plentiful and cheap; so are the crayfish, which are very similar to lobsters, when small, but the large ones rather coarse. I must not end my list of fish that we eat without mentioning one that is always ready to return the compliment when an opportunity offers, namely, the shark, many of whom are habitants of the bright tempting waters of Port Jackson. Provisions vary much in price from many circumstances. Everything was very dear when we landed in New South Wales, and at the present time prices are much too low to pay the producers.

The dust is one main source of annoyance in Sydney. Unless after very heavy rain, it is *always* dusty; and sometimes, when the wind is in one particular point, the whirlwinds of thick fine powder that fill every street and house are positive miseries. These dust-winds are locally named "brick-fielders," from the direction in which they come; and no sooner is the approach of one perceived than the streets are instantly deserted, windows and doors closely shut, and every one who can remains within till the plague has passed over, when you ring for the servant with a duster, and collect enough fine earth for a small garden off your chairs and tables.

Flies are another nuisance; they swarm in every room in tens of thousands, and blacken the breakfast or dinner table as soon as the viands appear, tumbling into the cream, tea, wine, and gravy with the most disgusting familiarity. But worse than these are the mosquitoes, nearly as numerous, and infinitely more detestable to those for whose luckless bodies they form an attachment, as they do to most new comers; a kind of initiatory compliment which I would gladly dispense with, for most intolerable is the torment they cause in the violent irritation of their moun-

tainous bites. All houses are furnished with a due attention to
these indefatigable gentry. and the beds have consequently a
curious aspect to an English eye accustomed to solid four-posters,
with voluminous hangings of chintz or damask, and a pile of
feather-beds which would annihilate a sleeper in this climate.
Here you have usually a neat thin skeleton-looking frame of
brass or iron, over which is thrown a gauze garment, consisting
of curtains, head, and tester, all sewn together; the former full,
and resting on the floor when let down, but during the day tied
up in festoons. Some of these materials are very pretty, being
silk, with satin stripes of white or other delicate tints on the
green gauze ground. At night, after the curtains are lowered,
a grand hunt takes place, to kill or drive out the mosquitoes from
within; having effected which somewhat wearisome task, you
tuck the net in all round, leaving one small bit which you carefully raise, and nimbly pop through the aperture into bed, closing the curtain after you. This certainly postpones the ingress
of the enemy, but no precaution that my often-tasked ingenuity
could invent will prevent it effectually. They are terrible pests,
and very frequently aided in their nocturnal invasions of one's rest
by the still worse and thrice-disgusting creatures familiar to most
dwellers in London lodgings or seaport inns, to say nothing of
fleas, which seem to pervade this colony in one universal swarm.
The thickest part of a town, or the most secluded spot in the
wild bush, is alike replete with these small but active annoyances.

One day we drove out to the lighthouse on the South Head,
about eight miles from Sydney. Soon after leaving the town
the road passes the new court-house and gaol, and its handsome
front, in the Doric or Ionic style (I forget which), is the only
architectural building the "city" could boast when I was there,
though I suppose that ere this the new Government House, a
mansion in the Elizabethan-Gothic style, is completed. We
began shortly to ascend a hill, the road being all sea-sand apparently, and nothing but sand was visible all around. Great green
mat-like plats of the pretty *Mesembryanthemum æquilaterale*,
or fig-marigold, adorned the hot sandy banks by the road-side.
It bears a bright purple flower, and a five-sided fruit, called by
children " pig-faces." A very prickly species of solanum also grew
here, with large green spiky leaves, more difficult to gather even

than holly, and pretty bluish potato-like blossoms. The universal tea-tree, and numberless shrubs which I knew not, adorned the sandy wastes in all directions. As we continued to ascend, the road became very rough, huge masses of rock protruding like gigantic steps, over which the wheels scraped and grated and jumped in a way that made me draw rather strong comparisons between the character of roads at home and abroad. As we approached the summit, the hollow formed by the road was suddenly filled by a background (forgive the paradox) of deep blue water; it was the open sea that gradually rose before us, seen over the rocks, and spreading out bright and blue, with small waves sparkling in the fervid sunshine, and the white diamond-crested spray dashing high against the iron-bound coast, here broken into a low craggy amphitheatre, into which the rolling waves came surging on, breaking over the groups of rocks, and forming bright little basins among them. On either side the rocks rose again in large masses, presenting a precipitous face to the sea, being part of the dark formidable cliffs we had seen in approaching the Heads by sea. The road, after descending the hill, turned to the left, through some sandy scrub, crowded with such exquisite flowers that to me it appeared one continued garden, and I walked for some distance, gathering handfuls of them—of the same plants that I had cherished in pots at home, or begged small sprays of in conservatories or greenhouses! I had whole boughs of the splendid metrosideros, a tall handsome shrub, bearing flowers of the richest crimson, like a large bottle-brush; several varieties of the delicate epacris; different species of acacia, tea-tree, and corræa, the brilliant " Botany-Bay lily," and very many yet more lovely denizens of this interesting country, of which I know not even the name. One, most beautiful, was something like a small iris, of a pure ultra-marine blue, with smaller petals in the centre, most delicately pencilled ; but ere I had gathered it five minutes, it had withered away, and I never could bring one home to make a drawing from. Surely it must have been some sensitive little fay, who, charmed into the form of a flower, might not bear the touch of a mortal hand !

Numbers of parrots, those

> " Strange bright birds, that on starry wings
> Bear the rich hues of all glorious things,"

were flying from tree to tree, or crossing the road in chattering, screaming parties, all as gay and happy as splendid colours and glad freedom could make them. Often they rose close before us from the road, like living gems and gold, so vividly bright they shone in the sun; and then a party of them would assemble in a tree, with such fluttering, and flying in and out, and under and over; such genteel-looking flirtations going on, as they sidled up and down the branches, with their droll sly-looking faces peering about, and inspecting us first with one eye, then with the other, that they seemed quite the monkeys of the feathered tribes.

On nearing the lighthouse, after ascending one or two slight hills, we passed several small houses, and others were building; the views from thence are doubtlessly very grand, but it must be a most exposed situation, with nothing to break the force of the strong sea-breezes, and but little vegetation to moderate the glare of the sun.

The view from the cliffs is indeed grand,

" O'er the glad waters of the dark-blue sea;"

and looking down over the dizzy height, the eye glances from crag to crag, till it catches the snowy puffs of foam flung up from the breakers that roar and dash in the cavernous chasms below, booming among them like subterranean thunder. As I fearfully gazed down, something leaped between me and the dark water—it was a goat, and there were some half-dozen of the agile creatures far down the slippery precipitous crags, leaping, jumping, and frolicking about, with scarcely an inch of foot-room, and only the boiling surf below.

Opposite to us rose the corresponding cliff, called the North Head, bluff and bare, and wearing on its hoary front the hues with which thousands of storms have dyed it. Myriads of sea-fowl were soaring and screaming around, and several vessels in the offing, and nearer shore, were apparently shaping their course to the port, but too distant for us to wait their entrance through these most grand and stupendous gates. The lighthouse itself is not in any way remarkable; close by is the signal-staff, by means of which the intelligence of vessels arriving is speedily transmitted to Sydney and Paramatta.

We drove back by a different road, nearer to the port, and less hilly, but equally beautiful with that by which we came. It

led us through a moister-looking region, with more large trees,
greener shrubs, and more luxuriant herbage, and commanding
most lovely views, that appeared in succession like pictures seen
through a natural framework of high white-stemmed gum-trees
and tall acacias. Here and there peeped forth a prettily situated
residence, with its shady garden and cool piazza, looking down into
one of the small bays I have before mentioned, and beyond that
to the estuary.

On one large dead gum-tree a whole council of black cockatoos
was assembled in animated debate, sidling up and down the
branches, erecting and lowering their handsome gold-tipped top-
knots, as if bowing to each other with the politest gestures imaginable; and accompanying the dumb show with such varied
intonations of voice as made it impossible to doubt that a most
interesting discussion was going on, all conducted in the most
courteous manner: perhaps a reform of the grub laws was in
agitation, for the business was evidently one of grave importance,
and we respectfully remained attentive spectators of the ceremony
until "the House" adjourned, and the honourable members flew
away. These birds are by no means common in the neighbourhood of Sydney, nor did I see any more during my stay in the
colony.

The same deep sandy road continued: it appeared to me that
this part of the country must have been gradually elevated from
the sea, and a long succession of beaches consequently formed,
and left inland by the retreating waters; for the prodigious
accumulation of true sea-sand here seems difficult to account for
in any other way. In the Domain, too, and many other situations,
are raised beaches, consisting wholly of sea-sand and shells
(recent ones, so far as I examined them), above which, in a thin
stratum of soil, great trees are growing; so that, although these
beaches have formed part of the dry land long enough for a body
of soil to be deposited upon them, and for aged trees to have
grown in that, they are still of modern elevation.

Sydney boasts her "Hyde Park;" but a *park* utterly destitute
of trees seems rather an anomaly. It is merely a large piece of
brown ground fenced in, where is a well of good water, from
which most of the houses are supplied by means of water-carts.
There is also a racecourse between the town and Botany Bay,

racing being a favourite amusement among the gentlemen of the colony, and sometimes among the ladies, for I was told of a race somewhere "up the country," in which two "young ladies" were the riders, the prize being a new side-saddle and bridle, which was won in good style by one of the fair damsels; the horse of the other receiving a severe castigation from his gentle mistress, for having swerved and lost the race.

Most of the country gentlemen near Sydney, and for many miles round, are members of the "Cumberland Hunt;" they have a tolerable pack of hounds, and the destructive native dog, or dingo, serves them for a fox. So long as they hunt the really wild ones, the sport is certainly useful; but when, as frequently happens, a *bagged dog* furnishes the day's amusement, I cannot but think the field of mounted red-coats as something less than children. Dinners and balls of course form a part of the arrangements for the races and hunts, and everything is conducted in as English a manner as can be attained by a young country imitating an old one.

There are several large churches in Sydney, plainly, but substantially built; and one was in progress when we were there, which promised a more architectural appearance. The Bishop of Australia is a resident in Sydney. The Roman Catholics, and various dissenting congregations, have also neat and commodious chapels.

I heard that there was a Museum of Natural History; and the "Australian Library" contains an excellent selection of books for so young an institution. The circulating libraries are very poor affairs, but, I fear, quite sufficient for the demand, reading not being a favourite pursuit. The gentlemen are too busy, or find a cigar more agreeable than a book; and the ladies, to quote the remark of a witty friend, "pay more attention to the adornment of their heads *without* than *within*." That there are many most happy exceptions to this rule, I gladly acknowledge; but in the majority of instances, a comparison between the intellect and conversation of Englishwomen, and those of an equal grade here, would be highly unfavourable to the latter. An apathetic indifference seems the besetting fault; an utter absence of interest or inquiry beyond the merest gossip,—the cut of a new sleeve, or

E

the guests at a late party. " Do you play ?" and " Do you draw ?"
are invariable queries to a new lady-arrival. " Do you *dance* ?"
is thought superfluous, for everybody dances ; but not a question
is heard relative to English literature or art ; far less a remark
on any political event, of however important a nature :—not a
syllable that betrays *thought*, unless some very inquiring belle
ask, " if you have seen the Queen, and whether she is *pretty* ?"
But all are dressed in the latest known fashion, and in the best
materials, though not always with that tasteful attention to the
accordance or contrast of colour which an elegant Englishwoman
would observe.

The natives (not the aborigines, but the " currency," as they
are termed, in distinction from the " sterling," or British-born residents) are often very good-looking when young ; but precocity
of growth and premature decay are unfortunately characteristic
of the greater portion. The children are mostly pale and slight,
though healthy, with very light hair and eyes—at least such is
their general appearance, with of course many exceptions. They
grow up tall ; the girls often very pretty and delicate-looking
whilst young (although very often disfigured by bad teeth) ; but
I have seen women of twenty-five or thirty, whose age I should
have guessed to be fifty at least. They marry very young, and
the consequent " olive branches " are extremely numerous. The
boys grow up long, and often lanky, seldom showing the strong
athletic build so common at home, or, if they do, it is spoiled by
round shoulders and a narrow chest, and, what puzzles me
exceedingly to account for, a very large proportion of both male
and female natives *snuffle* dreadfully ; just the same nasal twang
as many Americans have. In some cases English parents have
come out here with English-born children ; these all speak clearly
and well, and continue to do so, whilst those born after the
parents arrive in the colony have the detestable snuffle. This
is an enigma which passes my sagacity to solve.

Of course a large proportion of the population are emancipists
(convicts who have served their allotted years of transportation),
and their families or descendants ; and a strong line of demarca-
tion is in most instances observed between them and the free
emigrants and settlers. Wealth, all-powerful though it be,—

and many of these emancipists are the richest men in the colony,—
cannot wholly overcome the prejudice against them, though
policy, in some instances, greatly modifies it. Their want of
education is an effectual barrier to many, and these so wrap
themselves in the love of wealth, and the palpable, though mis-
placed importance it gives, that their descendants will probably
improve but little on the parental model. You may often see a
man of immense property, whose wife and daughters dress in the
extreme of fashion and finery, rolling home in his gay carriage
from his daily avocations, with face, hands, and apparel as dirty
and slovenly as any common mechanic. And the son of a similar character has been seen, with a dozen costly rings on his
coarse fingers, and chains, and shirt-pins, glistening with gems,
buying yet more expensive jewellery, yet without sock or stocking to his feet; the *shoes*, to which his *spurs* were attached, leaving a debatable ground between them and his trowsers! Spurs
and shoes are, I imagine, a fashion peculiar to this stamp of
exquisites, but among them very popular.

Many instances occur of individuals of this class returning to,
or perhaps for the first time visiting England, with the purpose of remaining there to enjoy their accumulated wealth, and
after a short trial, coming back to the colony, heartily disgusted
with the result of their experiment. Here, as " small tritons of
the minnows," they are noted *by* their riches, and courted
for them; but at home, shorn of their beams by the thousands
of greater lights than their own, and always subject to unpleasant prejudices and reflections touching " Botany Bay," and
other like associations, they find their dreams of grandeur and
importance wofully disappointed, and gladly hasten with all
speed from the scenes of mortified vanity. One of these
adventurous worthies made the voyage to England, landed, and
remained in London a very brief space,—not more, I believe,
than one or two weeks,—when, fully satisfied, he took ship and
set forth back again. On arriving in Sydney, his friends inquired his opinions of England;—Did he not admire the magnificent buildings and streets in London? " Oh! very well; but
nothing like George-street!" At all events, the extraordinary
perfection and beauty of the English horses *must* have delighted

him?—" No, not at all; nothing to be compared with Mr.
Cox's breed."

The good people of Sydney have yet many wise things to learn,
and many silly ones to unlearn, before they can attain that resemblance to the higher middle classes at home which is their
anxious aim; and the shallow petty pride, or rather vanity,
which causes so many heart-burnings and such eager rivalry
among those who can often but ill afford its cost, is the main-
spring of their follies. The existence of such feeling in a colony,
where all, with very rare exceptions, have sprung from needy
emigrants or transported criminals, is too absurd to require a
comment. Yet pride, of a right kind, *might* be the best agent
a new country could possess; but it must be a generous, not
selfish pride; it must strive for renown in a general good, not an
individual aggrandisement; it must show a wise and liberal, not
(as is too much the case at present) an ignorant and sordid
spirit; its effort must be, not to rise above its neighbours, and,
if possible, thrust them lower still, in contrast to its own exalta-
tion, but aid, by an example of strict integrity and honour,
careful industry, increasing knowledge, and true morality, the
interests of the community at large.

The distinctions in society here remind me of the "Dock-yard
people," described by Dickens, that keen and kindly satirist of
modern follies. Thus—Government officers don't know merchants; merchants with "stores" don't know other merchants
who keep "shops;" and the shopkeepers have, I doubt not, a
little code of their own, prescribing the proper distances to be
observed between drapers and haberdashers, butchers and pastry-
cooks. The general character of the invitations to the entertain-
ments at Government House has caused much discussion and
animadversion; the citizens who drive chariots not liking to be
mingled in company with their tradespeople who only keep gigs.
But all this pride of place is so very ridiculous and unbecoming
in such a community, that were not its tendency so mischievous,
it could only provoke a smile.

English customs and fashions are carefully followed, and frequently outdone by the more wealthy and (if I may be allowed
the phrase, in speaking of commoners) *aristocratic* of the colo-

nists.　Their extravagant mode of living, combined with the mania for speculation, has greatly contributed to the late and still existing embarrassments of the colony.　Many of their houses are elegant villas, with rooms of noble dimensions, expensively furnished with almost every luxury to be found in a gentleman's residence in England, and environed by beautiful gardens, where every description of fruit, both European and tropical, is cultivated.　The numerous servants too are a great and universal expense.　The smaller houses of merchants, and various professional and official men, have much the style of those in suburban streets in England, standing alone or in pairs, all protected from the sun by verandas from six to twelve feet wide, with pretty gardens in front, often fenced by high hedges of gay geraniums.　Several of these villa-streets are very pretty, and a most refreshing contrast to the dust, dirt, noise, and closeness of the lower part of the town, which is, from the climate and other causes, some shades more unpleasant than any place I ever was in before.

These rambling " Sketches" of mine are fortunately not required to be a complete " Guide" to all the lions, wonders, and beauties of Sydney and its vicinity, for of many I am totally ignorant.　I know it possesses a pretty theatre, and that frequent concerts and public balls are given at all seasons ; but as my health did not allow of my partaking in any amusement which demanded attendance in close and heated assemblies, I cannot speak of them from experience.　Three annual " national" balls were given whilst I was in the colony, which those present described as very gay affairs ; the tutelar saints of the three kingdoms being made patrons extraordinary on the occasion—St. George presiding over the English ball, St. Andrew over the Scotch, and St. Patrick, that " gentlemanly" saint, over the Irish entertainment. A fourth ball was then arranged, being a combination of the forces, and at this fancy dresses were very generally worn, and some well supported.　All these balls were very numerously attended, it being quite a matter of course for families to come above two hundred miles, even in that climate, and over *such* roads, to attend a ball.　How any one at home would laugh at the idea of journeying an equal distance on a like errand! even with all the aids of rail and turnpike-roads, stage-coaches and post-chaises! But young ladies are so numerous, and balls so comparatively rare, that it seems an act of policy not to lose these occasional opportunities for the display of charms that might otherwise " waste their sweetness on the desert air."

There are several good inns in Sydney, much frequented by bachelor settlers, and one, to which the married ones take their families, at about double the expense of accommodation in a first-rate English hotel; and whilst you are served with " King's pattern " plate, and by half a dozen waiters, you miss many of the commonest comforts to be found in every wayside hostel at home. These and similar inconsistencies are perpetually striking a new-comer, in every circumstance of life and every grade of society.

A stranger cannot fail to notice the prodigious number of public-houses in this place, and, judging from general appearances, I fear they are only too well supported, and receive the greater part of the earnings of the lower classes, among whom habits of intemperance are unhappily very prevalent. The advocates of the temperance and tee-total societies have, I believe, effected considerable good, but much more remains to be done.

My readers doubtless remember the inimitable passages in ' Pickwick,' descriptive and illustrative of the " Eatanswill Gazette," and " Independent," with their rival editors, Mr. Pott and Mr. Hurk. It is my sincere opinion that some of the colonial editors here have mutually resolved on attempting an exact imitation of the style and manner of these renowned papers, for their leading articles bear a most curious resemblance, fraught with the most deadly hatred of each other, and the same unmeasured powers of abuse and wholesale condemnation. Such terms as " Our base and mendacious contemporary ;" " That tissue of ignorance and conceit, the —— ;" " That mean-spirited creature, whose vile insinuations we despise ;" together with torrents of " rascal, liar, scoundrel, booby, fool, venom, viper, toad," &c. &c., give an indescribable piquancy and interest to their charming productions ; their brethren of Port Phillip,

Hobarton, &c., often zealously emulating their spirit and incomparable choice of language; though some are of a very different stamp, and, strange to say, are preferred by many persons who have the curious taste to peruse with more satisfaction European news, and quiet discussions of general topics, than the most fluent and animated harangues of these eloquent opponents.

CHAPTER VII.

IN the last chapter I have given my general impressions of Sydney; the result of our entire residence in the town and neighbourhood, rather than a mere first view, which could only observe the surface of things, my first sojourn there being only for a fortnight, when, our baggage being landed and stored, and all other arrangements completed, we prepared for a journey " up the country." My husband required to visit his sheep-stations on the Murrumbidgee; but my travels were not to extend farther than Bathurst, about 120 miles.

Our first day's journey was merely an afternoon drive to Parramatta, fifteen miles from Sydney, through alternate cleared land and " bush," but all enclosed. The chief of the way-side houses were those of publicans, round which drays and carts were usually assembled, whilst their drivers refreshed themselves within, and swarms of flies added to the torment and weariness of the miserable horses and oxen, who often wait for hours the return of their brutal and drunken guide.

The system of " clearing " here, by the total destruction of every native tree and shrub, gives a most bare, raw, and ugly appearance to a new place. In England we plant groves and woods, and think our country residences unfinished and incomplete without them; but here the exact contrary is the case, and unless a settler can see an expanse of bare, naked, unvaried, shadeless, dry, dusty land spread all around him, he fancies his dwelling " wild and uncivilized." About some of the older houses in the colony a growth of fruit-trees, and often British forest-trees, has succeeded the despised aboriginal productions, and sometimes a few of the grand Norfolk Island pines tower above the lower groups. Ungrafted quince and peach trees form hedges in many places; and when not hidden in the thick coat of dust which covers everything near a public road, their greener hue is a pleasing change amidst the brown landscape. Where land is not required for the plough, the trees are frequently only cut down within a yard of the ground, which remains thickly encumbered with the ugly blackened and burned stumps, giving the appearance at a little distance of a large and closely occupied graveyard; grubbing, or taking up the roots, being a far more expensive operation. Many large trees are destroyed by a ring of bark being taken off the trunk, when they die in the course of a year, and their huge leafless skeletons have an indescribably dreary and desolate aspect.

Maize, or Indian corn, which I here saw growing for the first time, is a most ornamental crop, each plant being placed by itself, and its long, broad, green leaves and crowning spire of blossoms having a very graceful appearance. It is generally cultivated here in lieu of other grain, for which the climate is less adapted, and is always understood by the term *corn*, all other corn, such as wheat, barley, &c., being called grain.

The habitations of the working classes, for *poor* there are none, are the least pleasing objects one meets with in this colony. Instead of the neat clean cottage of an English labourer, with its little glazed windows, and tidy though old curtains looped on one side; its small garden-plot of vegetables, pot-herbs, and sweet flowers, and cheerful, though humble aspect,—here you pass a wretched hut or hovel, built of heaped turf, or more frequently of "slabs" (rough pieces of split timber, set on end, like a strong paling), and thatched, and which, if plastered with mud, would be weather-proof and comfortable; but, for the most part, the slabs are all falling asunder, the thatch half torn off, the window, or rather the place for one, stopped with pieces of wood, hides, and old rags; and the door, without hinges, inclining against the wall. A heap of ashes and chips usually lies in front; broken bottles, old casks, old rags, bones, and shoes, and various similar articles are scattered around. Not a herb, not a cabbage is to be seen; no attempt at making a garden, although a fence might be had for the trouble of cutting it, and, by very little labour, abundant crops of vegetables and fruit produced. Unfortunately, at the time I speak of, wages were so high, that by working only a third or fourth part of his time, a man could gain an ample livelihood, and consequently those disposed to be idle had both time and money to spend in drunkenness ; the improvement and comfort of their homes had no share in their thoughts ; and the wife in many cases was as bad as her husband ; whilst the unfortunate children, growing up without instruction, and under such examples, cannot be expected to adopt any very moral or religious ideas. The rate of wages is no doubt now much lowered by the increased number of emigrants ; and this, by compelling many to acquire more industrious habits, will do immense good. I remember the wife of a turnpike-keeper near our house, who was scarcely ever seen sober, and as rarely without a broken head or a black eye. One day Mr. Meredith was driving a friend to the races at Parramatta, and, on reaching the turnpike, this engaging female was discovered seated at a table by the door, with a cup and a half-gallon bottle of rum beside her, the effect of which was already evident ; she offered Mr. Meredith a ticket, which he told her was not required, as she knew him so well from his passing constantly—" Oh, sir, you'd better take it, for I shan't know anybody by the time you come back !"

It is amusing enough, in traversing this colony, to come upon a spot in the midst of the wild bush, where a great finger-post stands to inform you that you are in the " township " of Monmouth, or Rutland, or some other old country name, with other posts at certain distances, bearing the names of streets, squares, &c., where not the semblance of a human dwelling is visible, though all arrangements seem made for a large and populous town. These, I imagine, are some of the " town allotments," in which such extensive and fatal speculations have been made in all parts of the colonies.

We passed several " chain-gangs " working on the road ; these are convicts, who, from their great and repeated crimes, are sentenced for various periods to work in irons in the service of the government ; and the villainous countenances of the greater number, the clank of their chains, and the thought of how awful an amount of crime had led to this disgraceful punishment, made me positively dread passing or meeting a band of the miserable

wretches. Very erroneous opinions relative to the state of convicts in these colonies exist at home as to the degree of hardship
they endure. I think I can in the course of these pages relate
enough from my own observation, to prove how much very many
humane persons are misled in their ideas on the subject. Even the
chain-gangs, the lowest grade of this class, do not perform on an
average the third part of the labour which any English mechanic
or labourer does gladly and cheerfully. Their rations of food are
wholesome and abundant, and their huts or barracks provided
with every necessary. When sick, they have the best medical care,
and whatever additional luxuries their state may require; and
when I apply to them the term " miserable wretches," I would
be understood as applying it to their crimes and social degrada-
tion, not to their corporal sufferings. They work under the super-
intendence of overseers, and sentinels with loaded muskets, who
would shoot any one attempting to escape ; but notwithstanding
every precaution, they do frequently evade the vigilance of their
guards, and, " taking the bush," that is, running away into the
forests, they often become formidable in their attacks on travellers in the lonely roads up the country. Not long ago, I saw an
account of *eleven* murders having been committed by one of these
desperadoes, and accompanied by such horrors of mangling, burning, and otherwise disposing of his victims, as far exceed all the
fearful tragedies of a like kind we read of in the English papers.
Several parties of bushrangers were out at the time of our journey, but as that is generally the case, it made no difference in our
arrangements.

Parramatta is a straggling and extensive place, with good wide
streets, containing houses and shops of every size and description,
which are most agreeably diversified by the pretty gardens en-
compassing many of them, shadowed with fine mulberry, orange,
and fig trees, and gay with luxuriant shrubs and flowers, among
which the large American aloe forms a prominent feature, and
frequently one appears in bloom. From its low situation, Parramatta is many degrees warmer than Sydney, and though seated
on the shores of Port Jackson (here called the Parramatta river),
it feels little if any benefit from the sea-breeze, which in Sydney
is so great a relief. I may here add another link to the chain

of antipodean absurdities enumerated by Mr. Baron Field,* by asserting that all the rivers are creeks, and all the creeks rivers; thus you hear people continually talking of the Parramatta *river*, which is neither more nor less than the higher portion of the estuary of Port Jackson, and perfectly salt : whilst if by chance you meet with a precious little stream of fresh water far inland, rest assured it is nothing but a " *creek*." I was most amusingly puzzled by hearing of " creeks" far away from the coast, and began to suspect my geography to be in fault, when I soon found them to be what in England we should call a brook or rivulet. Orange-groves and vineyards are numerous in the vicinity of Parramatta, and supply the " metropolis " with the chief of its fruit. Various kinds of oranges are grown, both sweet and bitter; among the latter, a very small one, called the mandarin orange, is a pretty and fragrant fruit, and makes a delicious preserve. The lemons are very different from those used in England, being much the shape of an ill-formed Seville orange, but well-flavoured and juicy.

Some of the houses are covered with vines, and the verandas of others richly tapestried with jasmine, woodbine, roses, and climbing plants of every description. The church is a singular-looking edifice, having two blunt spires, one of which only is surmounted with the usual vane and weathercock. The Court-house has a handsome Grecian portico of cut stone, and the " factory," or house of correction for female prisoners, the hospital, schools, and other public institutions are large establishments,

---

* " It is New Holland—where it is summer with us, when it is winter in Europe, and *vice versâ;* where the barometer rises before bad weather, and falls before good ; where the north is the hot wind, and the south the cold ; where the humblest house is fitted up with cedar (*Cedrela Toona*) ; where the fields are fenced with mahogany (*Eucalyptus robusta*) ; and myrtle-trees (*Myrtaceæ*) are burnt for fuel ; where the swans are black, and the eagles are white ; where the kangaroo, an animal between the squirrel and the deer, has five claws on its fore-paws, and three talons on its hind-legs, like a bird, and yet hops on its tail [It is almost needless to say that *this* absurd idea has long been exploded.—L.M.]; where the mole (*Ornithorhynchus paradoxus*)lays eggs, and has a duck's bill ; where there is a bird (*Melliphaga*) which has a broom in its mouth, instead of a tongue ; where there is a fish, one half belonging to the genus *Raia*, and the other to that of *Squalus ;* where the pears are made of wood (*Xylomelum pyriforme*), with the stalk at the broader end ; and where the cherry (*Exocarpus cupressiformis*) grows with the stone on the outside."

but I never was within any of them, although subsequently residing in the neighbourhood for some time.

After passing a particularly pretty garden, in which stood a long low house, with a spacious piazza in front, I was surprised by Mr. Meredith's driving up to the door, and still more so on finding that this was our inn, where we had engaged rooms. My belief that it was a private residence was natural enough, for the sign of the " Red Cow " on the roof had escaped my notice; but we were most comfortably accommodated in every way. The garden was full of beautiful flowers, particularly the bright scarlet blossoms of the pomegranate, the soft and fragrant oleander, and quantities of pink and crimson china-roses. An enormous prickly-pear (*Cactus opuntia?*) grew near the house (I think it must be twenty feet high), and was full of yellow blossoms and dark red fruit, in picking up some of which to taste, I stuck my gloves so full of the fine penetrating prickles that it was some days before I extracted them all from my hands.

Two beautiful birds were living tame in the garden ; they were called curlews, but I doubt if correctly. They were much the shape of the avosetta, with long straight legs, long straight bill, a prettily-marked brown plumage, and the finest eyes I ever saw in any but the eagle or hawk tribe. The female was very shy, having had her nest and eggs repeatedly destroyed by mischievous boys and visitors; but the male was ·very familiar, following us all about, uttering a plaintive cry, which I afterwards used to hear frequently at night near our own residence, where they were very numerous, though scarcely ever seen.

Several of the native parrots were caged in the veranda, and talked a little; one kind, as large as the grey and green parrots so often seen in England kept as pets, had a most elegant plumage, the back, wings, and upper part of the tail being pale lavender-colour, and the breast and tail-*linings* the most delicate pink. Beside these hung the prison of a lovely little creature, called the Bathurst parrot or parroquet, or, as I named it then, and have done ever since, the " painted lady," as on each cheek (or whatever ornithologists call the part of a bird's face which corresponds to that human feature) there is a round spot of soft crimson orange-colour; the rest of the fair lady's attire being bluish lavender, with a pale primrose-coloured breast; a long tail, and

pretty sly eyes, make her one of the most beautiful of this numerous and gay tribe of birds. In the streets, too, we met a
" native companion," or gigantic crane, walking about perfectly
tame and fearless, being a sort of general pet among the inhabitants ; he was between three and four feet high, and his enormous
bill, keen eyes, and grave demeanor gave him a most sapient and
dignified appearance as he stalked along, peering about, and sometimes pausing before one of the shop-doors, to take a more minute
survey of matters within.   But the chief glory of Parramatta
in the bird-line is now, alas ! no more.   This was a tame mag-
pie at one of the inns, of whose fluent conversation and wonderful ventriloquism I have heard most surprising stories, but I
never saw the prodigy myself.

On quitting Parramatta the following day, we passed near
Government House, which is beautifully situated in a fine domain, and frequently visited by the governor. Sir Maurice
O'Connell, commander of the forces in Australia, now resides
there.   The road to Penrith passes occasionally through pleasant
scenery, though chiefly monotonous enough, and the intense heat
made me almost incapable of enjoying anything ; added to which,
the indescribable chirruping, creaking, and whirring of myriads
of grasshoppers (*dust*-hoppers more properly), that seemed to fill
all space around us, was almost intolerable ; and what was very
extraordinary, these unwelcome musicians were wholly invisible,
nor could the most rigid observation detect them.   They seemed
to be a little below the surface of the loose dusty soil, and ceased
their noise when I approached them. I afterwards detected some
of their kindred at Bathurst, at least the voices were the same,
and found them to be insects of the true grasshopper shape, with
small wings, and about an inch long ; but these colonies swarm
with an immense variety of these long-legged insects of all sizes,
from a quarter of an inch to two inches in length, and of all
colours ; brown in every shade (particularly the tints of withered
grass and dead gum-leaves), green of the brightest hues, grey,
black, reddish, and purple. Many of the large ones are very
handsome and curious creatures.

Penrith is a long village, containing a few pretty, and many
new, raw-looking houses, profusely adorned with green paint on
the windows, shutters, verandas, and railings, and some had

very nice flower-gardens in front. We drove through the town to an inn some distance beyond it, close to the ferry over the Nepean, the first *river* I had seen in the colony, and the only one I did see there. The fine view of the Blue Mountains, rising beyond the level Emu Plains on the other side the river, beguiled me into walking in a garden on the banks till driven away by the clouds of mosquitoes; and as we sat in the veranda after dusk, I observed a single bright fiery spark glancing swiftly about in front of the house, now rising high into the air, and again falling, darting quickly to and fro, and occasionally resting a few seconds. On inquiry, I was told it was a fire-fly; but I was not aware that the bright creatures were found in New South Wales, nor did I ever observe more than this one.

I was told of an amusing incident which occurred to a new arrival during our stay. The traveller in question, putting on a most important aspect, walked into the stable, where the ostler was busy in his various duties, and pointing to a horse, inquired if he had been fed. "Yes, sir." "Give him another feed now directly." It was done. "Now, ostler, let that horse be ready for me at six o'clock to-morrow morning. Do you hear?" "*That* horse, sir? That isn't your horse, sir!" "No? Then which *is* my horse?" The steed was pointed out, and the proprietor departed. "Who is that person?" asked Mr. Meredith of the grinning functionary. "Can't say, sir; but I reckon he's a gen'leman wot's newly cotched!"

Early the following morning we resumed our journey, in company with a friend with whom we had arranged to travel the remainder of the way. Ourselves, carriages, and horses were safely ferried over the Nepean in a large punt, or railed raft, and landed on the opposite bank, when we drove merrily along the Emu Plains, so named no doubt from the flocks of emu formerly found there; but as civilized, and therefore doubly destructive, man advances in a new country, he invariably exterminates or scares away the timid creatures that have for ages dwelt there undisturbed; and now these noble birds have become unknown, except in the almost untrodden districts of the interior. I saw two tamed ones in a part of the government domain at Sydney; they are most noble-looking birds, and seemed quite happy in the comparative freedom they enjoyed. Their eggs are of a rich dark-green colour, with a rough surface, like the rind of a coarse orange, or shagreen, and are about the size of those of an ostrich, which bird the emu resembles in general appearance, though handsomer and less awkward.

We had a fine view of the long range of the Blue Mountains before us, and of the abrupt gorge through which the Nepean flows before reaching Penrith. This pass is described as being extremely grand on a nearer approach, as indeed it must be, from the perpendicular height of the mountains, and the large volume of water pouring through so narrow a channel.

After driving for about two miles over the level plains, we reached the foot of Lapstone Hill, the first ascent, up which an excellent road has been made, winding along the side of the mountain, with high overhanging rocks on the left hand and a deep wooded ravine on the right. The wild scenery and the zigzag road reminded me of some of the " passes of the Alps," as drawn by Brockedon, save that our ravine had no foaming torrent roaring down it; and it was only by most intent observation that I could detect something like moisture trickling over the rocks, where an opening in the trees left the far-down stony bed visible.

It was October, and, as I have before remarked, the spring months are by far the *greenest* in this land of ever-browns; so that I saw the country under rather favourable circumstances, although the severe droughts of the two preceding years had destroyed the artificial crops, and even the native grasses, to a deplorable extent. Still, among these lofty mountains and in their shady recesses the trees and shrubs grew in unchecked luxuriance, and yielded me many a new and beautiful flower. As we slowly wound up the steep ascent, and the folding hills narrowed the view behind us, the scene was most picturesque and striking. Far on before us we could see the white-gleaming road still climbing higher and higher; looking back, the plains, reduced to a triangular section by the closing hills, were fast receding from the landscape ; gigantic crags, piled high overhead, were mingled with an endless variety of tree, shrub, and flower ; and far below, from the depths of the ravine, the opposite side of the pass rose almost perpendicularly, till its upper trees seemed to cut against the bright, unclouded, blue sky. I was quite delighted, and thought that if all our progress over the dreaded Blue Mountains were as pleasant and interesting as the commencement, the journey would be much less wearisome than I anticipated.

I had often been told of the " waratah" (*Telopea speciocissima*), and its grand appearance when growing; and as we drove along, instantly recognised from the description the first of these magnificent flowers we saw, and soon after came more into their especial region, which is about half-way up the height of the mountains, few being seen either far above or below this range. From the temperature, I should think their cultivation at home would be easy, and it would well repay some pains to have such noble flowers added to the treasured wealth of English gardens. The stem is woody, and grows perfectly straight, from three to six feet in height, about the thickness of a walking-cane, and bearing rich green leaves (something like those of the oak, but much larger) all the way up. At the top of this stem is the flower, entirely of the brightest and richest shade of crimson-scarlet. A circle of large spreading petals forms its base, from which rises the cone or pyramid of trumpet-like florets, three, four, or five inches high ; the whole flower being much the size and shape of a fine artichoke. Sometimes the stems branch off like a candelabrum, but more generally the flowers grow singly, one on each stalk, and look like bright flambeaux amidst the dark recesses of these wild forests. Unfortunately I had no opportunity of making a drawing of one, having no materials at hand on our journey, and failed to procure a flower during our stay in Sydney. The few plates I have seen give but a very faint idea of this most stately and regal flower.

CHAPTER VIII.

A "Country Inn"—Breakfast—Contrasts—A Bush Ramble and digression about Ants—Mountain Scenery—Cattle-skeletons—" Weather-board " Inn —Supper and Night at "Blind Paddy's"—Mountains and the Surveyor's Roads—Mount Victoria—Convict-gangs and Bush-rangers—Inn at the " Rivulet " and its Inhabitants—The ruling Vice.

AFTER driving for some miles nearly all up-hill, we stayed to breakfast at a small way-side public-house, where the slovenly slipshod women, dirty floors, and a powerful odour of stale tobacco-smoke, gave me no very favourable expectations of cleanliness or comfort. On the smoke-stained walls hung some very highly coloured and showily framed prints, representing young gentlemen with red cheeks and very blue coats trying to look very hard at young ladies in pink gowns with very large sleeves ; and severally inscribed, " The Faithful Lovers ;" " The Betrothed ;" " The False One," &c. ; ingenious distinctions of character, which it would have been extremely difficult to discover from the portraits alone.

In many places you find some particular dish more generally in vogue than others, but in New South Wales one universal reply follows the query of " What can you give us to eat ?" and this is, " 'Am an' eggs, Sir ;" " mutton-chops " forming the usual accompaniment, if required. So ham and eggs we had, and mutton-chops too ; but from their being fried all together, in the same dark-complexioned fat, the taste of these viands was curiously similar, and both of impenetrable hardness. Unless great care is taken, meat spoils so soon in this climate, that the custom among most persons is to cook it almost as soon as killed, which of course precludes the possibility of its being tender. Tea, with black sugar, but no milk, and bread without butter, completed the repast, with the addition of " damper," a composition respecting which there are divers opinions, some persons preferring it to bread, whilst I think it the worst way of spoiling flour. The etymology is perhaps " Dampier," this indigestible food (an excellent damper of a good appetite) being supposed by some persons to have been invented by the great circumnavigator, and the manufacture is this:—A stiff dough is made of flour, water, and salt, and kneaded into a large flat cake, two or three inches thick, and from twelve to eighteen broad. The wood-ashes are then partially raked from the hot hearth, and the cake being laid on it, is heaped over with the remaining hot ashes, and thus bakes. When cut into, it exceeds in closeness and hard heaviness the worst bread or pudding I ever tasted, and the outside looks dirty, if it is not so: still, I have heard many persons, conversant with every comfort and luxury, praise the "damper;" so I can only consider my dislike a matter of taste. In " the bush," where brewer's yeast cannot be procured, and people are too idle or ignorant to manufacture a substitute for it (which is easily done), this indurated dough is the only kind of bread used, and those who eat it constantly must have an ostrich's digestion to combat its injurious effects.

At the period of which I am writing, wheat in Sydney had reached the exorbitant price of 10*l.* 16*s.* per quarter, to which every mile of distance from thence added cost, and this naturally induced every one to economize flour as much as possible; accordingly ground maize, boiled rice, and other things were added to the bread for this purpose, making it hot, bitter, or unpleasantly moist, as the case might be, but I do not remember seeing one instance of the flour being used unsifted, as it is in so many families at home, from motives of health or preference, although it might have been so used at such a time of dearth with manifest advantage.

Adjoining to this comfortless habitation (called an inn) was a small plot of potato-ground, but no attempt at neatness or improvement was visible; all was slovenly and neglected. The dirt and indescribable combination of ill smells within, was but a type of the state of things without. In the rear of the house one vast undistinguished rubbish-heap spread around, bounded only by some wretchedly dilapidated outhouses and stables, and reeking with foul exhalations, on which, and its more tangible delicacies, a large conversazione of pigs seemed to luxuriate most satisfactorily. Several children were lying or lounging about in

close companionship with the pigs, equally dirty, but apparently
less lively. Miserable creatures! I thought of the contrast between
them and children in a similar station at home, for this wretched
place would rank with the " Lion " or " Traveller's Rest " of a
country village in England, with its couple of clean white-draped
spare chambers, and its gay best parlour as neat and bright as a
new pin. The landlady, a rosy comely dame with a cap of
driven snow and smart flowered gown; the landlord, in cords
and blue stockings, velveteen coat, and sturdy figure, a *beau ideal*
of an English yeoman; and the children—most of them are at
school, but the rest, what clean, shiny, red, laughing, frolicsome
young rogues they are! Look on this picture and on that!
No—not again; so whilst my companions enjoyed their cigars in
the cobwebbed veranda, I crossed the road, and was at once
in the wild bush, where I rambled for some time, interested by
everything around me, though careful to keep tolerably near the
house. Strange birds were fluttering and whistling in the trees;
thousands of grasshoppers, large and small, leaped up wherever
I went, tumbling down again in their helpless way, with all
their legs abroad, and taking a few seconds to gather themselves
into place again for a fresh jump; myriads of ants, of various
sizes and species, were as busy as ants always are, running hither
and thither, up and down the smooth-barked gum-trees, in long
lines reaching from the ground far beyond my sight into the tall
branches; and here and there, near some old or fallen tree, a swift
little lizard would dart into his hole, giving me barely time
enough to see that he was not a snake, of which fearful creatures
I have a just and most intense terror.

In the course of this and the following day's journey we passed
many of the gigantic ant-hills common in some parts of New
South Wales. They are great conical heaps of finely worked
earth cemented into a hard mass, and from six to ten feet high,
with no visible orifice outside, nor did I see a single ant about
them, though I closely examined several. I have been told they
are the work of a white ant, and, from their magnitude, should
suppose them the habitation of a species of termite. When cut
open, they display numerous small cells, but on our journey I
had neither time nor inclination to destroy and investigate their
domestic arrangements myself. The earth of which these ant-

hills are formed, is so finely prepared by the little architects that it is used by the settlers in the neighbourhood as plaster, and frequently as cement for floors. Many various kinds of ants inhabit New South Wales and Van Diemen's Land; I know about a dozen species myself. One is a very formidable-looking personage, full an inch long, with a shiny coat of mail gleaming purple and blue, and a threatening sting, which I am told inflicts a most painful wound, as severe as that of the hornet. Besides these are several other large kinds, some entirely black, others with red heads, bodies, or legs. One, with black body and yellow forceps, not only acts on the defensive, but openly attacks any one passing too near him, by jumping at them, and stinging or biting severely; I have often been surprised to observe the distance they can spring when irritated or disturbed. Of the smaller kinds the numbers " are as the sands upon the seashore." They swarm in every part of the bush, and infest houses to an intolerable degree. In our house near Sydney, and also our present residence in Van Diemen's Land, I have been excessively annoyed by them ; not an atom of anything sweet can be hidden from their attacks : sideboard, pantry, storeroom, cellar, and kitchen, are all alike besieged by the industrious little torments. They bury themselves in sugar, and drown in jam, cream, custards, or tarts ; and their odour and taste are so indescribably nauseous, that their repeated visitations become rather expensive. Setting the forbidden viands in vessels of water seemed a perfect remedy, but still the ants gained access to them, and to my amazement I saw whole squadrons of the tiny black army deliberately marching across the water, and climbing the dishes within. Some particles of dust had no doubt fallen on the surface, and enabled them to step over dry. Ants are certainly most interesting creatures (always providing they preserve a respectful distance from one's grocery and sweetmeets), and in the bush I often watch them with great pleasure and without an idea of disturbing them. One day I observed a bright yellow circle on the ground, and on stooping to see what it might be, discovered a quantity of the golden-coloured petals of a small kind of cistus which grew near, neatly cut up into little bits (about the sixteenth of an inch wide), heaped all round an anthole, and crowds of my tiny household foes or their relatives busy

in various ways. Some were running about the low branches of
the cistus bushes, carrying fragments of the petals towards the
heap ; others, busy "getting in" the harvest, would come up
the hole, seize on a bit of the treasure, and, with the aid of
four or five more, pull it down below. Sometimes two parties
would bring their burden just to the opening at the same
moment, and as the passage was only wide enough for one
set at a time, a furious and determined struggle took place
as to which should first succeed, which, like many disputes
among larger animals, seemed to make up in violence what it
wanted in magnitude. I watched the indefatigable little creatures for some time, until I became quite cramped from my
crouching position, and still the same routine of business went on
with unabated activity.

"Mais revenons a nos moutons !"— We continued our journey
through a wild and barren country, utterly destitute of herbage ;
the inhospitable Blue Mountains were before, behind, and on
either side of us, rising in grand and dreary monotony of form
and colour. Forests of tall gum-trees covered them from base
to peak, but instead of a beauty in the landscape, these were a
deformity. All bore the marks of fire far up their branchless,
blackened stems, and in many places the burning had been so
recent, that for miles the very earth seemed charred, and not
even a stunted shrub had sprung up again. The trees, huge
masses of charcoal to all appearance, had no branches till very
near the summit, and these bore only a few scattered tufts of
rusty leaves, scarcely casting a visible shadow, and affording no
shade. The steepest ravines had not the semblance of water
in their dry dreary depths, and but for the fearful quagmires
and deep holes in the road (which made the utmost care in driving
requisite to avoid an upset over the precipice), one would not
have thought that rain or dew ever visited this desert region.

The main portion of the road is *bad* beyond an English comprehension ; sometimes it consists of natural step-like rocks protruding from the dust or sand one, two, or three feet above each
other, in huge slabs the width of the track, and over these
"*jumpers*," as they are pleasantly termed, we had to jolt and
bump along as we best might. How our springs stood such
unwonted exercise is an enigma still ; but as a vehicle of the ba-

rouche species, crammed in every imaginable corner with live freight and luggage, had passed the inn whilst we were at break-fast, I am inclined to think that springs in colonial use must be made of sterner stuff than I had hitherto given them credit for.

The track we were now traversing usually winds terrace-wise along the side of a steep mountain, and is barely wide enough any-where to allow of two vehicles passing each other. All the produce of the settlers in the upper country is conveyed to Sydney by this road, and farm supplies taken up from thence : therefore it is no uncommon thing to meet a train of six or eight heavily laden drays (for the continual depredations of bush-rangers render it advisable that several should travel in company), each drawn by eight, ten, or twelve oxen ; and to encounter such a caravan on the narrow mountain road is by no means a desirable incident. The patience and docility of the ox are justly proverbial, but un-fortunately colonial drivers are less gifted with these virtues, and their violence, ill-temper, and brutal usage often seem to bewilder the poor weary creatures, who, having no harness but bows and yokes, twist round and entangle themselves, much to their own peril and that of any passing horses or carriages. We once narrowly escaped a serious accident from this cause, by driving down the bank, steep as it was, out of the way.

Two years of desolating drought had preceded our arrival in Sydney, and the melancholy proofs of its ravages among the brute creation met us here at every turn, in the remains of un-fortunate oxen, that had perished of want in their toilsome journeys over the mountains, where neither food nor water re-mained for them ; and as the dray-journeys from the distant sta-tions to Sydney occupy from three to six weeks, the lingering, protracted misery endured, even by the wretched animals who survived, is horrible to contemplate. In some places by the road side white skeletons alone remained ; farther on we saw other car-casses still covered with hide ; then bones again ; and so on, con-tinually meeting these terrible proofs of the poor brutes' suffer-ings and death. It recalled to my mind descriptions I have read of the caravan-tracks in the sandy deserts of Africa, where the bleached bones of animals that have perished in the journey serve as guides to future travellers.

The climate changed materially as we gained the higher re-

gions of the mountains, becoming quite cold, and I gladly
wrapped up in cloaks and furs ; our companion, who usually drove
within hail of us, retired into a grotesque cloak-hood-and-coat
sort of a garment, made of the thick furry opossum-skins of the
Colony, and looked like an exaggerated Esquimaux, as we caught
a glimpse of his portly figure now and then through the thick
flurries of sleety rain that swept round us, the sudden squalls
being too furious for any umbrella to live in them. So, laughing
merrily (when the wind did not take our breath away), we drove
briskly on, our destination for the night being the "Weather-
board" inn (so named from its being built, like many houses in
the Colony, wholly of wood, the walls consisting of thin boards
lapped one over another, nailed to upright slabs or posts, and
lathed and plastered within). What was my dismay, as I was
just ready to alight, cold, tired, and hungry, at the door of this
mountain refuge for the destitute, on our being informed that
the house was full, and not a sleeping-place to be had ! A native
settler returning from Sydney to Bathurst with his wife and
family were in possession of all the accommodation. These were
the occupants of the loaded carriage I had seen, who, with more
foresight than ourselves, had pushed on as rapidly as possible in
advance, and seized upon the whole establishment. After a short
debate it was determined to go on six miles farther, to a smaller
hostel, known as "Blind Paddy's," though it was nearly dark,
and raining fast. However, on we went, "through bush and
through brier," to say nothing of holes and rocks in the road ;
and in process of time, long after dark, reached our little inn, very
wet, and colder and hungrier than ever. A couple of decent
elderly women appeared to do the honours, and ushered us into a
small but clean whitewashed room, gaily adorned with feathers,
shells, and the droll little pictures usually found in such houses :
a bright wood-fire was soon crackling and blazing merrily on the
white hearth ; the homely table was quickly spread with a coarse
but snowy cloth, and supper most expeditiously prepared, consisting of the never-failing dish " ham and eggs," chops, damper,
tea, and—crowning luxury of all—a dish of hot mealy potatoes,
smiling most charmingly through their cracked and peeling
skins. Wine in such houses as this is rarely drinkable, but excellent English ale (at 3s. 6d. per quart bottle) is generally found

in them, so that our repast was by no means contemptible, and the air of plain homely cleanliness about the arrangements added to all an unwonted relish.

A tolerable night's rest in a room about the size of our ship-cabin, with a clean dimity bed and window-curtains, and no worse nocturnal visitants than a moderate party of the universal "light infantry," left me quite recruited and ready for setting forth again on our onward journey, after a breakfast very similar to our supper, or rather dinner, of the preceding evening.

Our route still lay through the same wild, monotonous scenery as the day before. The sight of vast mountain-ranges spread all around, folding in and behind each other as if they filled all space, could not be otherwise than *grand* in the extreme, but it was most dreary, desolate grandeur. Trees without foliage, hills and valleys alike destitute of verdure, chasms and ravines yawning beside us, without a thread of water in their arid, stony depths, made up such a world of desolation, that the contemplation of it became absolutely oppressive, and I gladly listened to glowing descriptions of the green and beautiful plains of Bathurst, which we were to reach the following day.

In one place we came to an almost precipitous descent in the road, called "Soldier's Pinch," or "Pitch," most probably from some accident which has happened there. It was a mass of loose stones, continually rolling from under the horses' feet, and so steep as to be very fatiguing even to walk down, which I preferred doing, not being quite reconciled to such roads for driving on. At the foot lay huge masses and heaps of wood, trees of all sizes having been hooked on to the drays at the summit of the Pitch, to prevent their rushing down suddenly, despite locked wheels, and overrunning the unfortunate oxen. If Major Mitchell, when Colonial Surveyor, had turned his attention and directed his men's labour to such places as this, and remedied their dangerous character, he would have rendered great and essential service to the colonists; but in the generality of instances his road has been made where a *good* bush-track formerly existed, and the really bad and dangerous portions remain in very many instances untouched—at least such was the case when I crossed the mountains. I could not avoid noticing likewise, that Major Mitchell's road, wherever originally marked by him, was almost invariably carried over the summits of hills, whilst level valleys lay within a few hundred feet; and as we proceeded, I looked out for the highest peaks ahead of us, knowing by experience that the surveyor's road would lead us over them. I was informed that a determination to adopt no other person's suggested line of road was the reason of this most inconvenient and fatiguing route being resolved on, and I have since heard that a new survey is to be made, and a more level and rational track marked out.

The only portion of the present road for which I can give Major Mitchell great credit is the Pass of Mount Victoria, by far the most grand and striking scene in this mountain region. As we approached it, a huge barrier of rocks seemed to close up the onward path, till a sudden turn showed us a gorge cut in them, through which we drove, with a high wall of crags on the right hand and the lofty summit of the mount towering up on the left. Another turn brought us out of the chasm, and in full view of a most grand and beautiful landscape. The road was carried (from the opening of the chasm) by an arch and embankment across a deep valley that lay below, called the Vale of Clwydd, and along the side of the opposite mountain, till it gradually reached the level of the valley beyond. We stayed some minutes on the embankment to enjoy the prospect, so refreshing to eyes weary of the dark desolate sterility of the scenes we had just emerged from. On the left hand, the high rocky range of which Mount Victoria forms a part nearly enclosed the narrowing valley, the lower portions being overgrown with gum and wattle (*Acacia*) trees, amidst which grotesque rocks rose up here and there like fantastic ruins. From the deep watercourses that were plainly visible on the mountain-sides, the stream running through the vale must sometimes be considerable; but at the time we passed it was dry, and its tolerably green banks, shadowed by groups of graceful young gum-trees, had quite a smooth and lawn-like aspect as compared with the rough country around. On the right hand the same long range of precipitous rugged heights continued, stretching away to the northeast; and safely girdled by their fortress-like and frowning walls lay the pretty vale of Clwydd.

Clustering richly about the shrubs near Mount Victoria I first observed the lovely " native indigo" of New South Wales (*Kenne-*

dia ovata?). It is a delicate little climbing plant, with slender stems, long, narrow, blunt leaves, and a profuse quantity of small, violet-blue pea-shaped flowers, growing in long sprays, and completely clothing any bush or fence where it flourishes. We had alighted on the archway, to enjoy the view at leisure, and I, as usual, indulged my rambling and scrambling propensities by a descent into the ravine below, where I found many lovely flowering shrubs, including some dozen species of acacia, some of them very fragrant.

A large gang of convicts were stationed here road-making, and several of them importuned us for money or tobacco, showing such truly villainous countenances that the idea of being waylaid by bush-rangers gained tenfold horror, and the knowledge that many were out made me often look very earnestly at a misshapen gum-log or crooked tree, fancy transforming it to "a highwayman, with pistols as long as my arm." In one place, we met a couple of soldiers in search of some newly-escaped convicts; they were running about in a half-stooping position, peeping and thrusting their fixed bayonets into every thin bush and low tussock of grass where a man could not by any possibility be hidden, with most valorous resolves no doubt, but cutting rather a ludicrous figure. I am not aware if they succeeded in their chace, but have strong suspicions that they did not.

A comparatively level road succeeded to the grand mountain pass, and we journeyed on to our mid-day resting-place, called the "Rivulet," the little stream at this place being by some remarkable accident rightly named. A new, glaringly smart-looking inn here promised tolerable accommodation; it was as fine as twenty differently coloured kinds of paint could make it. Panellings and "pickings-out" of rainbow hues were set off by pillars of imitative and varnished marble, the like of which no quarry ever knew; and these again, touched up with bronze-paint and gilding, gleamed in the sun with almost dazzling lustre. A good veranda led by French windows to the two front rooms, into which I walked, without seeing any inhabitants or attendants. A few gaudily painted chairs, a small bad mirror in a large gilt frame thickly shrouded in yellow gauze, and a new cedar table covered with tobacco-ashes and liquor-stains, composed the furniture of either apartment. After a long and ineffectual sonata on the hand-bell (no other description being seen, save in a very few of the very best colonial houses), just as I began to despair of its power, a young girl shuffled along the hall from some of the back settlements, and holding fast by the door-handle, for she was almost too much intoxicated to stand, took my orders for luncheon, and after many vain attempts at length succeeded in wiping the table with a ragged, very dirty apron. Her dull light-coloured hair hung in matted tangles about her neck and ears; her dress was disordered, torn, and dirty; and her face bloated and stupid from the effects of drink;—never did drunkenness wear a more revolting aspect, and I felt relieved when the wretched creature left the room. My companions had a similar tale to tell of the male portion of the establishment; every soul was drunk, and it was some time before they could arouse any one to attend to the horses. The same unfortunate girl I had before seen, laid our cloth, and brought what we wanted, or rather what we could get, for I imagine the copious libations indulged in by the whole household had made them regardless of eating, and the larder was accordingly very ill supplied. Bread and a few eggs (positively without ham!), which our ministering Bacchante rolled on the floor as she staggered in with them, formed our repast, but she took pains to impress upon us the pleasing assurance that "There was plenty o' ale an' sperrits."

We strolled down to the banks of the little rivulet, where I found many beautiful flowering shrubs, and the verdure of the adjacent little flats showed how excellent a garden might be made there, but I fear never will; idleness and drinking are such besetting sins, and money to provide them both so easily earned by "keeping a public" in this Colony, that nothing demanding bodily exertion is attempted. Meat can run about and feed itself on the wild hills, and flour they can buy; fruit and vegetables they "don't heed," as they would demand some little labour to produce.

As we returned towards the house, I looked at it again, as it stood in raw, shiny, comfortless newness, like a great toy freshly unpacked. Behind it lay a crowd of dirty, old, ruinous hovels, that formerly served in its stead, and still were used as outhouses, stables, &c., all broken, and half unthatched. All the fences within sight exhibited the same dilapidated aspect, whilst ash-heaps and other less sightly things lay all around. How different would be the state of almost everything in this Colony, were that greatest curse man ever created out of God's good gifts, intoxicating liquor, less easily obtained by those who *ought* to be the industrious and prosperous, but, alas! too generally *are* the idle and worthless part of the community. Time, money, character, decency, feeling, principle, ambition, and honesty—all are sacrificed to the demoralizing passion for rum, when once it gains the ascendency; and to know how often that is, we need only observe and listen to the sad evidence so continually passing around us. I perhaps praise the tidy appearance and good cookery of a friend's servant : " Ah ! yes, she is an excellent cook, but we can so seldom keep her *sober*." The coachman of another seems quite a model for his class, till you hear he is so confirmed a drunkard that his mistress dares not trust him to drive her home alone from a party. Another family have an honest old " major-domo," faithful and good in every other point; may be trusted with " untold gold," but not with a bottle of rum. It is a universal failing, and a really sober servant or mechanic may consequently be held as a pearl of great price. Age and sex make no difference ; your dainty lady's-maid or pretty young nurse-girl is just as likely to be over-liberal in her libations to Bacchus as your groom or shoeblack ; and no threats, no bribes, no punishments avail to keep the besotted creatures from the dram-bottle, if it be by any means or in any shape accessible. I have known a female servant drink camphorated spirits of wine, and suspect the same individual of consuming a pint of hartshorn which mysteriously disappeared about the same time from my room ; its evident strength being no doubt too tempting. Eau de Cologne and lavender-water, I know, they drink whenever they are left about, or anything else believed to contain spirit. The universality of this vice is most dreadful to contemplate, and far worse to witness and endure. Almost the only exceptions among the lower classes are the families of English emigrants, who, accustomed to poor living and hard work at home, continue sober and industrious, thankful for the many hitherto unknown comforts and luxuries they can enjoy, and carefully and fearfully abstaining from all excess.   Of this class I have known excellent examples, both old and young, male and female, and can only hope that in time their better and wiser course may be appreciated and emulated by other portions of this now numerous population.

CHAPTER IX.

"Hassan's Walls"—Grass-trees—Mount Lambey—Victoria Inn—Specimen
of Benevolent Politeness—Colonial Bridges—First View of Bathurst—
The "Settlement"—Dearth—Climate—Hot Winds—Processions of Whirlwinds—Hurricanes.

OUR road now lay over hilly ground again, sometimes skirted by
live trees and a slight semblance of herbage, and often approaching in wild and sterile grandeur the scenery we had before traversed. A singular range of perpendicular cliffs form a striking
feature in the landscape at a place called "Hassan's Walls."
These walls or cliffs rise, I should think, to a height of about
300 feet perpendicularly above the road, and their summits,
broken and fissured in various fantastic forms, exactly resemble a
ruined castle crowning the brow of the sheer precipice, with
here and there a stunted tree or graceful shrub growing from
crevices in the dark rock. Had I been travelling in an old
country, I should at once have decided that these were truly the
ruins of some mighty mountain-fortress of former days; loop-
holes, arches, battlements, and buttresses were, as it seemed, so
clearly remaining, and extending far along the airy heights of
these genii-haunted crags, for such I half fancied them, especially
when a turn in the road gave to view a colossal head standing
well out against the clear, bright, blue sky, and bearing a
strong resemblance to the venerable and veteran Duke of Wellington. We paused to contemplate the rude though striking
likeness; and then, as we slowly drove on, the features changed,
and a judge with a flowing wig stood frowning down on us;
another turn, and another change came over the mountain statue,
and then it again resolved itself into a mere turret of the hoary

ruin. I thought of the mysterious castle of St. John,* with its
wizard transformations, and of how much romance would attach
to these fantastic crags in a romantic or legendary country ; but
the existence of poetry or imagination in New South Wales is
what none who know and have felt the leaden influence of its
ledger and day-book kind of atmosphere would believe it guilty
of suffering.

The grass-tree *(Xanthorrhœa arborea?)* is one of the most
strikingly novel plants I observed in our mountain journey, and is
common in most hilly or rocky places both in New South Wales
and Van Diemen's Land. A young grass-tree appears merely a
large reedy-leaved plant without a stem, the leaves being very
long, narrow, and sharp, and growing erect for a foot or more,
then curving over and nearly touching the ground, forming
a thick boss or circle ; but as the tree becomes older, the lower
circles of leaves drop off, the young growth all rising from the
centre; and in time a thick stem appears, from one to eight or
ten feet in height, and two feet in circumference, rough with the
scars left by the fallen leaves, and bearing on its summit an immense drooping cluster of foliage, which reminded me of a palm-
tree (although, it must be confessed, by rather a clumsy resemblance). From the centre of this cluster the scape rises like an
enormous bullrush or typha, frequently measuring ten feet and

* " Midmost of the vale, a mound
  Arose, with airy turrets crown'd,
  Buttress, and rampire's circling bound,
      And mighty keep and tower.
  Seem'd some primeval giant's hand
  The castle's massive walls had plann'd.
      *   *   *   *
  But the grey walls no banners crown'd;
  Upon the watch-tower's airy round
  No warder stood his horn to sound ;
  No guard beside the bridge was found ;
  And where the Gothic gateway frown'd,
      Glanc'd neither bill nor bow.
      *   *   *   *
      This dismal keep,
      Which well he guess'd the hold
  Of wizard stern, or goblin grim,
  Or Pagan of gigantic limb,
      The tyrant of the wold."
  For the magic and gramoury of the Castle, *vide* Sir Walter Scott's ' Bridal
of Triermain.'

more in height, the spike being about a foot long, of a yellowish brown colour. Groups of this very singular plant often give a picturesque and somewhat Oriental aspect to an otherwise uninteresting landscape, some being old, crooked and deformed, hump-backed and knobby; others erect and stately, bearing their verdure like a royal diadem; whilst the young ones, sitting close to the ground in all humility, look up to their patriarchal neighbours with the patient hope of one day rivalling their nobler growth. A resinous gum exudes from the grass-tree, said to resemble in great measure the " dragon's blood " prepared from the Pterocarpus and Calamus. Boiled with oil, it has, I believe, been successfully used for covering the bottom of vessels, instead of pitch. I have also heard that the natives cut out the pith of the trunk to eat.

The next point of our route having any claim to the picturesque was the rocky ravine at Cox's River; the sight of clear running water is always pleasant, but nowhere more delightful than in so dry and thirsty a clime as this. The ruins of numerous huts, formerly occupied by a convict-gang at this spot, gave it rather a desolate look; but the clear little brook (for such in England should we call this river) gurgling merrily over its pebbly bed, had a sweet music in its voice that made me forget all disagreeables. We tasted, and then crossed it, and immediately began the steep ascent of Mount Lambey, which rises abruptly from the river's bank. This mount had been the highest point in our landscape all day, and accordingly, despising all humbler and easier tracks, over its very summit passes Major Mitchell's vaunted road. Seven long miles of climbing were before us, up as bare, sterile a mountain as ever gloomed on a wayfarer's path. The rock is a splintery slate, not unlike many in old South and North Wales, and its dark grey and purple hue, stained in places with a rusty tinge, gave a dismal monotony to the scene, which scarcely a shrub or herb appeared to relieve.

An inn has very wisely been built half-way up this inhospitable mountain, and there, at the auspicious sign of the Queen Victoria, we purposed remaining the night, which was fast approaching, for the rapid departure of twilight leaves little time after sunset available for travelling. After a weary pull of four miles, the gracious countenance of our fair Queen (somewhat libelled by the artist, it is true) beamed on our most loyal and rejoiced eyes from amidst a chaos of crown, sceptre, red drapery, and ermine; and our tired horses, after a last resolute effort, stopped at the inn door. At the same moment we heard a hand-bell sharply and loudly rung within, and after a minute's delay the landlord appeared at our summons, with the pleasing intelligence that he was very sorry indeed, but he could not accommodate us. As it was impossible to proceed farther in this case, there being no other habitation within a long stage, and our horses knocked up, Mr. Meredith and Mr. Campbell declared their determination to stay at all events; and again questioned the landlord, who then admitted his own willingness to receive us (and who of his class ever voluntarily rejected good customers?), which he could easily do at some trifling inconvenience, but Mrs. —— (whose party had the preceding evening excluded us from the " Weather-board ") was there, and the instant we stopped had *ordered* that no one else should be admitted, as they had taken *all the house!* This most overbearing monopoly, however, did not prevent our being comfortably installed in a snug little parlour, and a tolerable bed-room, which some of the landlord's family vacated for us, whilst the sofa in the sitting-room was made up into a bed for our companion. I am well aware that had we been known at the time, the conduct of this " lady " would have been very different; but at such an hour, and in such a place, no woman possessed of common humanity would have desired to turn a beggar from the door. The pride of wealth, unmixed with aught of better or nobler feeling, is too often the sole and engrossing principle and characteristic of persons raised by some fortunate chance to that kind of rank which in these Colonies, where the worship of Mammon reigns triumphantly, is at once accorded to the *rich :* " What *has* he ?" not " What *is* he ?" being the test; and this petty superiority is often the foundation of absurd and selfish importance, of which the above trifling incident is an apt illustration.

I am happy to say we found the members of this royal establishment sober, industrious, and civil; a most welcome contrast to the inn at the Rivulet, and, despite our unpropitious reception, were tolerably comfortable.

The following morning we again set forth, and after completing the ascent of Mount Lambey, proceeded to descend its opposite side, a far more pleasing task, especially as the surrounding country gradually assumed a less wild and inhospitable aspect. There is one little peculiarity in Colonial bridges, at least those usually met with on roads like the one of which I am treating, which it may be proper to mention; namely, that it is always far safer to plunge into the stream, morass, or ravine they stretch across, and wade or scramble out the best way you can, horses, carriage, and all, than to trust their treacherous and far more dangerous conveniency, for, like the celebrated bridge planned by Jack the Giant-killer for the destruction of the two-headed Thundel, they are apt to part company just as the passenger has passed too far to recede. In one place I remember seeing men erecting a stone bridge, with strong, good masonry; but the usual contrivance of a few long poles, covered with turfs, is far from satisfactory.

We rested about mid-day at a tidy public-house, which, although the fair hostess is believed to suffer from the prevailing thirst after strong drinks, we found very neat and clean; the miniature apartments set forth with bright Birmingham tea-trays, conch-shells, and the beautiful tail of the lyre pheasant, whilst the whitewashed walls and dimity curtains preserved their purity most surprisingly in this fly-tormented country. We had experienced the effects of the drought in the exorbitant charges made for the horses at every place we stopped at; and here, for a few handfuls of bad hay, ten shillings were added to the other items of the bill.

Journeying on, we arrived in process of time at the spot whence the first view of those lovely and verdant plains of Bathurst, of which I had heard so much, was to greet my delighted eyes.

" There, look ! Do you not see them through the trees?"

I did look, anxiously and eagerly, directing my eye-glass towards every point of the compass in succession; still nothing green could I discern, but on a nearer approach beheld a wide extent of brown earth, with occasional flurries of dust passing across it; and this was all that remained of the so-vaunted Bathurst Plains ! Every blade of grass and every green herb had disappeared during the drought, and a dry desert usurped their place, whilst a few thin, weak, widely-separated little roots of dry,

withering everlastings (*Gnaphalium*) were the only things bearing the semblance of vegetation.   It was very dreary !

We drove along the tedious road across the plains, which just
undulate enough in places to prevent a person from seeing entirely over them, and that is all ; no hill, grove, or tree, scarcely
a bush, breaks the heavy, weary monotony, till the tired eye
rests on the dim outline of the distant hills.   At length a few
straggling houses and a church showed us that we approached
the settlement ; but as this is divided into two portions about a
mile asunder, with the deep channel which is sometimes (water
permitting) the river Macquarie between them, we had yet farther
to go.   The second division of the township contains the gaol,
police-office, female factory, barracks, Scotch chapel, and bank,
with several stores and small shops of a most heterogeneous character, where you may find iron pots, writing-paper, blonde lace,
fire-arms, Dutch cheese, " P. coats," crockery, and various other
commodities, though very rarely the one article you require.
The private dwellings are of all grades, but chiefly of the smaller
class ; and the public-houses, as compared with the others, very
numerous.

The bank, then the residence of near relatives, was our destination, and most welcome to me were the happy quiet and rest of
the next few days, after our not very long, but tedious and
fatiguing journey.

Bathurst, being the last township on the " up-country road," is
comparatively a place of some importance, and frequently visited
by settlers from the less civilized districts beyond, to whom
it is a kind of half-way metropolis, as well as being in their direct
road to Sydney, whence there is a mail-cart twice a week (the
distance being 120 miles) ; a strange-looking two-wheeled vehicle,
carrying the post, the driver, and two passengers when required.
Travelling both night and day, and over the chief part of the
delectable roads I have faintly described, at a hand-gallop, it is
not exactly the conveyance to be selected by nervous or comfortable persons.   How the whole concern escapes destruction, at
least once a week, seems miraculous ; but with the favourite bush
assurance of " No fear, Sir !" away they go, driving at the pace
of a hunt over ground that would make a steeple-chaser look
twice ; and if there be no fear, there is certainly far less danger

than might be supposed, for I do not remember hearing of above half a dozen accidents during our residence in the Colony.

We found Bathurst still suffering severely from the devastating and ruinous consequences of the terrible drought. Every article of food was extremely dear, and nothing good could be procured at any price. Meat was lean to starvation, and flour liberally adulterated with various cheaper ingredients ; vegetables there were none; butter and milk had long been but a name ; and all horse corn, hay, &c., so extremely scarce, and exorbitantly dear, that the neighbouring families had for some time ceased to use their carriage-horses, the poor animals not having strength to perform any work. The cost of a horse at livery was then one pound per night, and it had recently been two pounds. Visiting Bathurst under such peculiarly unfavourable circumstances, I could not be expected to form any very high opinion of its beauties or advantages ; every one told me how very charming a place it had always been, and so I am bound to believe it was, and may be again ; but as I saw it, the inevitable impression on my mind was of a most dreary and unpleasing character. Its position, in the middle of a large plain, some twenty miles across, combines many disadvantages, one of the greatest being the distance which all the fire-wood used in the settlement has to be brought, and its consequent high price ; one pound being given for a small load, which in most places in the Colony, where it costs nothing, would not serve for more than a winter day's consumption in a moderately-sized household (indeed I believe *more* is burned in our kitchen alone), but here a much greater economy is necessary ; and as the cold is often as extreme here in winter as the heat is in summer, the scarcity of fuel is a serious evil.

I found the climate of Bathurst still less pleasant than that of Sydney, as in the latter place, however oppressive be the heat, the mid-day sea-breeze moderates it in some degree ; but the plains of Bathurst (although considerably elevated), being shut in on all sides by lofty ranges of mountains, must endure without any relief their own oven-like atmosphere, the temperature of which is frequently increased tenfold by a " hot wind," when it seems as if a fiery blast from a huge furnace pervaded all space around, rushing into the house through every opening with the force of a hurricane. My English habit of flinging wide open all doors and windows in warm weather, I here found (as a matter of course, so near the antipodes) a most imprudent course to pursue, as the only chance of preserving a moderately endurable existence during the continuance of the sirocco is, immediately on its approach to shut every door and window, and with closely-drawn blinds to await, as patiently and movelessly as half-suffocated mortals may be expected to do, the abatement of the terrible visitation. With us, however, a few hours of faintness, thirst, and misery generally comprise the whole evil (though sometimes the hot winds blow almost without intermission for several days), but the luckless fields and gardens escape not so easily. Every green thing looks as if a salamander had been held over it, either drooping and dying, or dried up like half-burned paper. I have seen large tracts of cultivated land, covered with luxuriant green crops of wheat, barley, or oats just going into ear, scorched, shrivelled, absolutely blackened by the heat, and fit for nothing but to cut as bad litter. Less important, though extremely vexatious, is the destruction caused in gardens, where the most delicate and beautiful flowers are ever the first to wither under the burning breath of this fervid Air-king.

These siroccos always blow from the north-west, and by some persons are supposed to derive their heat from tracts of unknown deserts in the intertropical regions of this island-continent. Their power is felt strongly, though less frequently, in Van Diemen's Land. One might almost fancy the Ancient Mariner to have experienced one during his ghostly voyage, he so accurately describes their aspect :—

> " All in a hot and copper sky
> The bloody sun at noon
> Right up above the mast did stand,
> No bigger than the moon."

I several times observed at Bathurst a phenomenon by no means unusual on the large plains of New South Wales, in dry weather, being a procession across them of tall columns of dust—whirlwinds in fact, which preserve a nearly uniform diameter throughout their whole length, the upper end seeming to vanish off, or puff away like light smoke, and the lower apparently touching the earth. They move in a perpendicular position, quietly and majestically gliding along one after another, seeming, at the distance I saw them, to be from seventy to a hundred feet high, and about twenty broad. Thus viewed, they do not appear to travel particularly fast, but Mr. Meredith tells me he has vainly endeavoured to keep pace with them for a short time, even when mounted on a fleet horse. When they are crossing a brook or river, the lower portion of the dust is lost sight of, and a considerable agitation disturbs the water, but immediately on landing the same appearance is resumed. As some vanish, others imperceptibly arise, and join the giant-waltz; and when I first observed this most singular display, I amused myself by fancying them a new species of genii relaxing from their more laborious avocations, and having a sedate and stately dance all to themselves. When the dance ends, these dusty performers always appear to sit down among the neighbouring hills.

I never heard of these gregarious whirlwinds being at all mischievous; they only pick up dust, leaves, little sticks, or other light bodies, which whirl round in them with great velocity; but other and far more terrible visitations occur in the hurricanes, which, like those of the western world, devastate the tract of country over which they pass. Mr. Meredith, in returning from his visit to the Murrumbidgee, encountered one of the most fearful of these terrific tempests. At Bathurst on the same day we had a violent thunder-storm, with a heavy fall of rain and large hailstones, but the fury of the tempest passed chiefly near the river Abercrombie. I shall avail myself of my husband's observations in his own words:—

"I have often seen the effects of former hurricanes in New South Wales, the indications being the total destruction of all trees in the course the hurricane had taken, which course I generally observed to be from the north-west. The length to which the devastation extended I had no opportunity of estimating, but the breadth averaged from 400 to 800 yards. On one occasion I saw the spot where a hurricane had terminated in a whirlwind. My companion and myself had ridden for some distance along the path it had pursued, the direction of which was plainly indicated by the trees it had uprooted in its course all lying one way; the termination was as plainly shown by a circle, in which the trees lay *all* ways; and such is their partiality, or rather, so clearly are the boundaries of both hurricane and whirlwind defined, that in cases where the blast did not reach the trunk of a tree, the branches were torn off from one side, without uprooting the stem.

"In the beginning of November, 1839, I was journeying from Goulburn to Bathurst by the direct route of the Abercrombie river, through a wild country, covered almost entirely with forests of very lofty gum-trees. On my departure from Mr. M'Allister's station in the morning, the wind was blowing strong, and the sky betokened tempestuous weather. As the day advanced, the gusts of wind became more and more violent, occasionally bringing down the branch of a tree. When I had arrived within three or four miles of the Abercrombie river the air became suddenly warm, and a few flashes of vivid lightning accompanied by loud thunder denoted the approach of a storm. A strong instinctive sensation of fear came over me, such as I never before experienced; and in a short time, perhaps a minute, I heard a strange, loud, rushing noise; the air grew rapidly dark and thick, and my horse was evidently, like myself, under the influence of intense fear, and trembling violently. I exclaimed (although alone), 'This is a hurricane!' and jumped off my horse at the *end* of a fallen tree; the poor animal endeavoured to shelter himself by backing under a growing tree, which I prevented by a violent pull at his bridle, and then for the space of a minute or two saw nothing; the hurricane, for such it was, had reached me, and everything was in total darkness. I fell on my knees, still holding my horse's bridle. The roaring, crashing sound was deafening, but it soon passed by, and the atmosphere again became clear enough to admit of my observing surrounding objects. My horse and myself stood alone in what a few seconds before had been a high and dense forest; every tree was prostrate, either broken or uprooted, including the one from under which I had luckily pulled my horse, its ponderous trunk lying within a few feet of us. Fortunately the track of the hurricane was in the same direction as that in which the fallen tree lay at the end of which I dismounted, and thus the small space was left which saved us both. Immediately that the hurricane had swept by, the rain fell in torrents, exceeding anything I ever witnessed in the tropics, and a heavy gale continued for two days."

The horse Mr. Meredith had with him then, a beautiful creature, and a great favourite, retained an evident recollection of
his terror in the hurricane long after—indeed, until we parted
with him, on leaving the Colony. If a branch of a tree only
lay before him in the road, or a twig blew across him, he
would look fearfully at it, start, snort, and tremble, which, as
he never used to notice such things before the occasion above
mentioned, we believed to be the result of some remembrance or
association in his mind. Perhaps the term *mind* is wrong as
applied to a brute, however noble in nature, but this evident
memory seems something above instinct.

CHAPTER X.

Bathurst Society and Hospitality—" White Rock "—Native Dance and Cere-
mony—Kangaroo Dance—Appearance of Natives—Children—" Gins;"
their marriage-slavery and sufferings—Family Dinner-party—Adopted
Children—Infanticide—Religion—" Devil-devil "—Language—Story of
Hougong and Jimmy—" Ay, Ay?"—Duties of the Toilet—Native Songs—
Mimicry—Fondness for English Dress—Boundary Laws—Legal Parricide
—Habitual Treachery.

IT savours strongly of an Irishism to say so, but the chief
inhabitants of Bathurst live at some distance from it ; many of the
wealthy, and also higher class of settlers, having farms and good
residences within a few miles, which renders the society superior
to that of Colonial settlements in general.   Nearly all are situated on the verge of the plains, combining both the flat and hilly
country in their surrounding scenery, and their gardens and vineyards, which at the time we were there were slowly recovering
their former verdure and luxuriance, seemed morsels of a brighter
world, when compared with the arid waste around the township.
Among these the pretty and picturesque residence of our good
and venerable friend Captain Piper is as much distinguished by
its beautiful situation as by the long-proved worth and hospitality
of its owner, than whom I heard of no person in New South
Wales more universally respected.   Hospitality is so general a
feature in Australian society, and I remember with so much
pleasure the kind attentions which I, as a " stranger in the land,"
received for my husband's sake, that only a very remarkable pre-
eminence would induce me to break my prescribed rule of abstaining from all personal allusions in these pages.

About three miles from Bathurst, near a pretty cottage on the
Macquarie (in a district chiefly granite), is a singular group of
low rocks rising abruptly from the turf of the plains, and perfectly white ; they appeared to me to be masses of pure quartz,
of which many specimens occur a few miles higher up the river.

Pebbles of very clear quartz crystal are sometimes found in the neighbourhood, but the natives search for them so successfully, that I only picked up one or two small ones. These crystals, although by no means rare, are preserved as " charms " by the Aborigines, being given to them by their doctors, or " Crodjees," after a variety of ceremonies, which Mr. Meredith describes to me as highly absurd, he having been present at the rites, when performed by a tribe at Dundunemawl on the Macquarie, about forty miles below Wellington Valley. Great preparations were made, as for a grand Corrobbory, or festival, the men divesting themselves of even the portions of clothing commonly worn, and painting their naked black bodies in a hideous manner with pipe-clay. After dark they lit their fires, which are small, but kept blazing with constant additions of dry bark and leaves, and the sable gentry assembled by degrees as they completed their evening toilettes, *full dress* being painted nudity. A few began dancing in different parties, preparatory to the grand display, and the women, squatting on the ground, commenced their strange monotonous chant, each beating accurate time with two boomerangs. Then began the grand corrobbory, and all the men joined in the dance, leaping, jumping, bounding about in the most violent manner, but always in strict unison with each other, and keeping time with the chorus, accompanying their wild gesticulations with frightful yells and noises. The whole " tableau " is fearfully grand : the dark wild forest scenery around—the bright fire-light gleaming upon the savage and uncouth figures of the men, their natural dark hue being made absolutely horrible by the paintings bestowed on them, consisting of lines and other marks done in white and red pipe-clay, which give them an indescribably ghastly and fiendish aspect — their strange attitudes, and violent contortions and movements, and the unearthly sound of their yells, mingled with the wild and monotonous wail-like chant of the women, make altogether a very near approach to the horribly sublime, in the estimation of most Europeans who have witnessed an assembly of the kind. In the midst of the performance on this occasion, two men advanced, bearing between them a large piece of bark, about six feet high and three feet wide, rudely painted with red and white clay, the design consisting of a straight line down the middle, and diagonal ones thickly marked on each side. The exhibition of this wonderful and mystic specimen of art caused extreme excitement and admiration, and the bearers held it in the midst of the dancers, who bounded and yelled around it with redoubled energy. Presently the oldest " Crodjee" present approached the charmed bark, and walked slowly round and round, examining it in every part, and then carefully smelling it, up and down, before, behind, and on all sides, with grave and reverential demeanour. This was to " find where the charms lay," which charms, consisting of small crystals, he had of course concealed about his person. After a great deal of smelling and snuffing, he commenced violently sucking a part of the bark, and, after some other manœuvres, spat out a " charm" into his hand, and went on sucking for as many as were then required.

These charmed crystals are kept with great care by the possessor, his wife usually having charge of the treasure, which she carries in the family " wardrobe," and the loss of one is esteemed an awful calamity. The charm-sucking ceremony takes place at the full moon, the time generally chosen by the natives for such celebrations. In this instance the Crodjee's part of the performance was very clumsily done, and Mr. Meredith asked one of the men, the following day, " if he were such a fool as to believe that the Crodjee really sucked the crystals out of the bark?" The fellow winked, nodded, and looked wondrously wise, and intimated that *he* certainly *knew* better, but that it would not do to *say* so. And thus is fraud perpetuated, alike by savage and by civilized men, and thus ever do policy and expediency take the place of truth and honesty !

One of the aboriginal dances is called " the Kangaroo dance," and one man, wearing a long tail, drops down on his hands and feet, pretending to graze, starting to look about, and mimicking the demeanour of the animal as nearly as possible ; the others, in the character of dogs and hunters, performing their part of the play in a circle round him, at a very short distance.

The natives I saw at Bathurst were less ugly and better proportioned than I expected ; the men being far superior to the women, though none of them are tall or largely made ; six feet is a most extraordinary size among them. The sable picanninies were naked, long-armed, large-stomached, little bodies, giving one the idea of a new sort of spider; I never had seen a black child before, and did not see enough of them then to familiarize me with the novelty. Several of the men knew Mr. Meredith, and whilst I was one day making some purchase in a store, one of them accosted him at the door, pointing at the same time to me. " Lady there, that Gin 'long o' you?—Ay, Ay?" " Yes, that's my Gin."—" Ay, Ay?" Then somewhat banteringly, " Bel you got Gin (you have no Gin); poor fellow you—you no Gin!" A "poor fellow" meaning a bachelor, and the possession of a wife, among them, being in fact equivalent to keeping a servant, as the unfortunate Gins perform all the labour.

Judging from what I have heard, I imagine that their marriage-customs are as truly *savage* as any other of their strange ceremonies. Polygamy is general among all who can attain the desirable wealth of several wives, though few have more than two living with them at one time.

Female children are sometimes "promised" in infancy to their future husbands (frequently decrepit old men), and others appear to be taken by means of force and ill usage, as is the case among many savage nations. The men are always tyrannical, and often brutally cruel to their unfortunate wives, who really seem to occupy as miserable and debased a position, in *every* respect, as it is possible for human beings to do. I never before heard of, or could have conceived, any state so pitiable and so utterly degraded. If some of the zealous Missionaries of whom we hear so much were to endeavour to raise the moral and social condition of these wretched creatures, and to teach them a few of the simple principles and virtues of Christianity, they would indeed be worthily employed.

Severe personal chastisement is among the lesser grievances of the poor Gins. One day Mr. Meredith saw one of them crying most bitterly, and asked what was the matter. She replied, that she was going to get a beating because she had accidentally broken her husband's " pyook " (pipe). Mr. Meredith directly went to the fellow, and tried to dissuade him from his brutal purpose; but in vain, unless another pyook were given him, on which condition he would let her off. Unfortunately there was not one to be procured; and notwithstanding all my husband's persuasions, and his representations to the black tyrant of the simple fact,

that even if he killed his wife, that would not make him a new
pipe, he remained doggedly sulky, and the next morning the
poor Gin appeared with her *arm broken*, from the cruel beating
he had given her with a thick stick. Such instances are of frequent occurrence.

These poor unhappy wretches are *slaves*, in every social sense,
and are not even permitted to feed but at their husband's pleasure, and off the offal he may choose to fling them, although on
them devolves the chief care of providing the materials for the
repast. Two meals a day is the full allowance of the natives;
but as they cook all they have for supper, and gorge themselves
then to their utmost ability, breakfast depends on the possible
remains of the feast. Their usual food consists of kangaroos and
opossums roasted whole, without any portion being rejected; and
they greedily devour garbage, entrails, &c. of any kind they can
pick up, quantity rather than quality being the desideratum as
regards provisions. Sometimes they feed more daintily, procuring turtle, fish, wild turkeys' eggs, guanas, snakes, and some
large kinds of grubs, which are reckoned great luxuries. Occasionally the women dig up a bitter hot root, not unlike a bad
radish, which serves them for a meal, in default of better
viands.

Each family have their own fire, round which they sit to eat.
The husband first takes the opossum, &c., tears it to pieces and
gnaws off his own favourite morsels from the joints, which he
then hands over his shoulder to his wife, who waits patiently
behind him; and should food be scarce, her supper is a tolerably
light one. The children are " helped" much in the same manner;
and when, either from having eaten as much as they can, or all
they have, the family have finished their repast, they crouch
round the fire and go to sleep.

The single men, emphatically termed " poor fellows," have
one fire in common; and with them, as with the family group, it
is a point of etiquette to hand round their half-gnawed bones to
one another.

Great fondness is usually displayed by parents for their children
(if they survive the perils of infancy), and instances have often
occurred of a couple, who had several little ones of their own,
adopting some poor friendless orphan, and freely bestowing on

it an equal share of their scanty food. Such cases I have known frequently among the *poor* at home : they who have least to give, and are consequently most intimate with the misery of want, have the greatest compassion and charity for fellow-sufferers.

Although they appear to treat their children kindly when they can in some measure help themselves, yet infanticide is frequent among the women, who often dislike the trouble of taking care of their babies, and destroy them immediately after birth, saying that " Yahoo," or " Devil-devil," took them. One woman, whom Mr. Meredith saw a day or two after the birth of her baby, on being asked where it was, replied with perfect nonchalance, " I believe Dingo patta !"—*She believed the dog had eaten it !* Numbers of the hapless little beings are ,no doubt disposed of by their unnatural mothers in a similar manner.

I never could make out anything of their religious ideas, or even if they had a comprehension of a beneficent Supreme Being ; but they have an *evil* spirit, which causes them great terror, whom they call " Yahoo," or " Devil-devil :" he lives in the tops of the steepest and rockiest mountains, which are totally inaccessible to all human beings, and comes down at night to seize and run away with men, women, or children, whom he eats up, children being his favourite food ; and this superstition is used doubtless as a cloak to many a horrid and revolting crime committed by the wretched and unnatural mothers, who nearly always, when their infants disappear, say " Yahoo" took them. They never can tell which way he goes by his tracks, because he has the power of turning his feet in any direction he pleases, but usually wears them heels first, or, as they express it, " Mundoey that-a-way, cobbra *that*-a-way" (feet going one way, and head or face pointing the other). The name Devil-devil is of course borrowed from our vocabulary, and the doubling of the phrase denotes how terrible or intense a devil he is ; that of Yahoo, being used to express a bad spirit, or " Bugaboo," was common also with the aborigines of Van Diemen's Land, and is as likely to be a coincidence with, as a loan from, Dean Swift ; just as their word " *coolar*," for anger, very nearly approaches in sound our word *choler*, with a like meaning.

I have seen a vocabulary of the language used by the native tribes near Adelaide, together with a few particulars touching their superstitions and customs,* but the words wholly differ from those used to express the same thing by the tribes about Bathurst, Goulburn, and the Murrumbidgee. I have been told by a friend of Mr. Meredith's, who had made himself thoroughly acquainted with many of the tribes, and was known among them as the " chief who spoke their tongue," that great diversity of dialects exists among them—not slight variations merely, but a distinctly different vocabulary, of which he gave me many striking instances. As my few examples of their patois will show, the natives who are acquainted with the settlers soon acquire a curiously composite tongue, where English words sometimes masquerade in most novel meanings, but so arranged as to be very soon understood, especially if used to beg anything.

In all the tribes some particularly solemn ceremonies are performed previously to a youth's being permitted to rank among the warriors, or " men;" but these take place in a very secret manner, not even the women being present. One of the initiatory rites, as practised among some tribes, is the knocking out one of the novice's front teeth.

The natives pay great respect to old age; that, and valour, comprising the only distinctions of rank allowed among them. The best fighting man is the chief or head of his tribe, and in case of his death, the next best takes his place, and inherits his wives. The other warriors and the old men form a sort of council, which is convened as occasion demands, when peace, war, and all other points of importance are discussed and decided upon.

A man named Hougong was some time chief of a Maneroo tribe, and another, called Jimmy the Rover, was second-best man. Jimmy mortally hated Hougong, but contrived to conceal his animosity under the mask of extreme friendliness, which, as his chief was no doubt as great an adept at hypocrisy as himself, was of little consequence. One day Jimmy went to a stockkeeper in the neighbourhood, to propose that he should ask them both to go duck-shooting, and requesting the loan of two guns, one of which should be loaded with ball, for himself, the other with powder only, for Hougong. " Well, me and Hougong go

* In a paper by John Philip Gell, Esq., of Hobart Town, published in the Second Number of the ' Tasmanian Journal.'

out look for duck, ay, ay. Bel make-a-light duck!—Den me
pialla Hougong—' Good many time you want fight along
o' me; *now* fight, like it white man, along o' musket.' Well, me
pialla—' You shoot first time.' Well, that fellow shoot. ' Ah!
you 'tupid fellow, bel hit it!' Den me shoot; directly tumble
down Hougong!"

Which notable speech, rendered into English, would be,
" Well, I and Hougong shall then go and look for ducks. Ay,
ay—we don't see any ducks. Then I say to Hougong, ' You
have wanted to fight me many times; let us fight now, like white
men, with muskets.' Well, I say, ' You shoot first.' He shoots.
—' Ah, you stupid fellow, you did not hit me!' Then I shoot,
and Hougong falls dead!"

Shortly after the failure of this most treacherous and cold-
blooded scheme of murder (for of course he was refused the
guns) Jimmy heard that Hougong was dead. Great were the
lamentations raised for their brave chief by his tribe, and most
vehement and vociferous of all were the howlings and groanings
of Jimmy the Rover. A friend of Mr. Meredith's, who was present at part of the mourning, found Jimmy full of public woe
and private exultation, venting the latter in theatrical *asides* to
those in his confidence, during the impetuous outpourings of his
tumultuous stage-effect grief, beginning at the top of his voice,
and howling most hideously down its whole gamut, more like the
yelling of a discontented dog than any other vocal performance
I am acquainted with.

" Oh! oh! oh! oh! Ooo-oo-oo-oo-ah! [Cabou (big) rogue that
fellow Hougong!] Oh! oh! oh! oh! Oo, oo, oo-oo. [Now he
dead, directly me maan (take) his Gins!] Oh! oh!" and *Da Capo.*

Accordingly, as soon as decorum and etiquette permitted, the
triumphant Jimmy prepared to go and take possession of his new
honours, when who should arrive, alive and well, but the defunct
and bemoaned Hougong himself!—and who, on hearing of
Jimmy's kind intentions, promised him a sound beating for his
pains.

The various expression conveyed by the peculiar " Ay, ay,"
so constantly used by the natives in speaking, is perfectly indescribable. It is used doubtfully, positively, interrogatively, or
responsively, as the case may be, and contains in itself a whole

vocabulary of meanings, which a hundred times the number of
words could not convey in writing. Suppose you inquire of a
native if he have seen such and such a person pass, as he has
gone that way :—" Ay, ay?" (interrogatively.) " Yes, a tall
man."—" Ay, ay " (thoughtfully). " A tall man, with great
whiskers." " Ay, ay (positively). Good way up cobbra, cabou
grasse ; ay, ay " (corroboratively).

" Good way up cobbra," means " head high up ;" *grasse* is used
to express hair, beard, or moustache ; and *cabou* means great
deal, or very much. The aborigines wear no beards themselves,
but a friend of ours, who had cultivated a most patriarchal
growth of that commodity, excited great awe and admiration
among them.

The labour and pains they bestow on their corrobbory toilets
prove them by no means insensible to the advantages of personal
beauty, although their manner of enhancing their natural charms,
in adding a thick stratum of pipe-clay to their usual coating of
grease and other accumulations, seems indeed " *as* wasteful and
ridiculous excess " as " to paint the lily, or throw a perfume
on the violet."   In lieu of

" Rowland's inestimable oil Macassar,"

their black elvish locks are always plentifully loaded with opossum or snake fat, which unsavoury unguent, as may be imagined,
adds its share to the powerful and not too-pleasing odour natural
to them.

A sable exquisite preparing for an evening party first undresses,
then thrusts a large lump of pipe-clay into his mouth to soften,
and when of a proper consistency uses his forefinger as a pencil,
dipping it into the composition, and carefully dispensing the
cherished ornament over his person. Having, with infinite regard
to the general effect of the pattern, accurately striped and crossed,
and wavy-lined and dotted every accessible part of his figure, he
selects a trusty friend on whom devolves the important and re-
sponsible office of finishing off the work of adornment ; and this
done, no reigning belle of the season ever entered Almack's
with more consciousness of all-powerful beauty than he feels in
taking his place among the equally elaborate costumes of his
companions. I fear the poor young squaws, or " Gins," have
but little to do with their own disposal in marriage ; but doubt-

less many a tender heart must be touched by these D'Orsays of
the wilderness; and many a pipe-clayed hero is painted in inde-
lible tints on the memory of love. My husband's animated and
pantomimic descriptions of these scenes have often made me
laugh heartily; but a second-hand detail must of necessity lose
much, if not all the interest.

The aboriginal songs which I have heard are far from unpleasing in sound, and some have considerable melody, with much
more tune and variety than those of the New Zealanders, which
surprised me, as the latter people are so immeasurably superior
to the natives of New South Wales in everything else. The
words which the latter sing usually celebrate some great feast,
nearly all being about eating. One (translated) runs nearly
thus:—" Eat great deal; eat, eat, eat: eat again, plenty to eat!
eat more yet; eat, eat, eat!" &c. &c.; and this is sung to a
rather plaintive, pretty air! Another song consists of a like
repetition of " Wind blow, blow; wind blow," &c.; the air being
really pretty. The events celebrated by these songs are seldom
of a very dignified description. On one occasion a bullock-
driver, known to some of a tribe, got drunk, fought his companions, and had a black eye, which occurrence was immediately immortalized by his black friends in a ditty, of which the
burden, chiefly English, was " Black-eye, black-eye," with repe-
titions endless, the remainder being in their own language. I
remember once hearing some one say of modern fashionable songs,
" What is the use of saying the same thing so many times over?"
but these native troubadours far exceed the most echo-weary of
drawing-room ballads, for, as I conceive, the self-same reason, a
lamentable paucity of ideas.

Most of the natives are shrewd and clever mimics; one learned
to waltz very correctly in a few minutes; and the slightest peculiarity of face or figure never escapes their observation, so that
in speaking of any person you know, although his name be not
mentioned, their accurate impersonation of his gait, expression of
countenance, or any oddity of manner, is so complete as to leave
no doubt of the identity. Their fondness for portions of European
clothing is well known, and I have heard of many amusing instances
of its display. One Wellington boot was sometimes worn, unac-
companied by any other article of apparel, and great was the pride

and grandeur of him who could button his upper man in a dress-coat, that alone being considered an ample costume. Other garments were subjected to various modes of wearing, for which they were never intended, legs being inserted where arms should be, and *vice versâ.*

The gift of a brass medal, formerly a rare distinction, is now made so frequently by settlers to natives who have served them well in any way, that the honour of the badge is somewhat diminished; but the pride with which the possessor wears and displays the insignia of his order is most amusing. The " medal " consists of a piece of brass in the form of a crescent, not much less than a cheese-plate, engraven with the name and style of both owner and donor, and worn hung round the neck by a brass chain.

Some of the native " attachés " to the establishments of settlers become useful servants, and are comfortably attired in suitable clothes, and their more than erect carriage (for a plumb-line dropped from the top of the head would fall some inches behind the heel) is still more striking in their civilized than savage costume. These men often accompany their masters' drays to Sydney, and sometimes join the long and toilsome stock-driving expeditions across to Adelaide; but even after a sojourn of many months with Europeans, and in a comparatively civilized state, they invariably return to their old habits, and relinquish their smart and comfortable clothes for the corrobbory costume of nudity and pipe-clay.

The companionship of natives in the overland journeys above alluded to might perhaps be supposed of service in preventing injury or attacks from other natives, but this is far from being the case. The whole of the aborigines, as hitherto known, maintain most rigid laws touching all boundary questions, each tribe having a certain allotted portion of country, beyond which they cannot pass but in peril of their lives, or at least without risk of a battle; and when, even in company with and under the protection of their white masters, they traverse these forbidden climes, and meet parties of the rightful inhabitants, the adventurous travellers manifest the most intense fear, which, judging from the threatening and angry aspect of their foes, is tolerably well grounded.

Neighbouring tribes are generally at war, some of the chief causes being acts of trespass and abduction of women; but the battles between them are less murderous than might be expected, all being great bullies, and perpetually vaunting of their grand resolves, and the numbers they mean to kill; whilst it often happens, that after their spears and boomerangs have been flying about for an hour or two, both armies quit the field with undiminished numbers.

A tolerable idea of their "manners and customs" may be formed from an occurrence which took place within Mr. Meredith's knowledge. An intimation being given by a neighbouring tribe to that settled near Goulburn, that they would kill a certain old man among the latter, a council was held forthwith on the subject, and means discussed how this indignity should be prevented; when, after much deliberation, the elders and fighting men decided on a most strange and horrible expedient, being that the old man's *own son* should kill him then, and so deprive their foes of the pleasure! The young man immediately rose, took two spears, and gave his miserable old father his death-wound as he sat, unconscious of any harm, by his fire, although it was some hours before he expired; his son meanwhile tending him with the utmost care and affection. After his death his son and the whole tribe mourned and howled over him several days; and then, taking their weapons, they set forth to go and kill as many as they could of the other tribe, to avenge the death of the old man. They were very successful, leaving several of their foes dead; but the police magistrate of Goulburn, annoyed by their fightings, threatened them with punishment, which caused them to set off in a large body, and well armed, on a peaceful visit to the Bathurst tribe, who received them with all honour and civility, and gave a grand corrobbory on the occasion, inviting the strangers to see them dance. The Goulburns accepted, but came armed with all their weapons; which Mr. Meredith observing, he asked them why they came to a dance armed as if for battle. They evaded the question some time, at length saying, " If we keep our weapons, very well, all go right; if we come without, directly they *jump up coolar* " (pick a quarrel, or get angry). A greater proof of the habitual treachery of these people could not be given than this distrust and suspicion of their own countrymen. From all I have heard, I am very much inclined to think my husband's maxim is the prudent one :—" Never *trust* a savage : you may serve them, and they may serve you ; but never give them the chance of an advantage."

CHAPTER XI.

Native Huts—" Gunyon "—Natives' ingenuity in Duck-snaring and Fishing
—Native Weapons—Green Frogs—Freshwater Shells—Platypus—Spur-
winged Plover—Australian Harebell—Convolvulus—Everlastings—Peppermint-tree—Opossums—Natives' Mode of taking them.

I HAVE often wondered that constant intercourse with Europeans, and experience of the comfort afforded by a permanent
and substantial shelter from the inclemency of the seasons in the
variable climate of New South Wales, has not induced the
natives to make some rude attempt at building themselves huts,
especially as they are always very glad to enjoy the benefit of
dwelling in those of the settlers. But their idleness is wholly
unconquerable; the uttermost effort they ever make towards
the formation of a residence being to raise a few strips of bark
slantingly against a tree, under which they crawl during bad
weather. Had not these primitive erections been pointed out to
me as "natives' huts," I confess I should not have had an
idea that they were anything more than accidental heaps of
bark.

One very wet miserable day a black was crowding in the warm
chimney-corner of a "squatter's" hut, where my husband was
present, and some of the party were asking the native why he
was so idle and stupid as to go shivering about without a home,
when he might soon build himself a warm hut. He listened very
quietly to all they had to say, merely observing at last, with
the air of a man who has arrived at a most philosophical conclusion :—" Ay, ay ! White fellow think it best that-a-way—Black
fellow think it best *that*-a-way." "Then black fellow 's a fool
for his pains," was the uncourteous rejoinder. "I believe so,"
returned the sable stoic, and straightway folding his blanket
around him, walked calmly out into the pouring rain.

A native one day was wistfully eying a snug pigsty, where

the fat grunting inmates were awaiting their supper, which was
being cracked in a mill by a convict servant; doubtless their
idle and obese condition must have seemed to him the *ne plus
ultra* of luxury, for he thus feelingly apostrophized the pigs:
" Ay, ay, budgeree fellow you! sit in gunyon all day—white
fellow grind for you !" (Ay, ay, you 're a lucky fellow, can lie in
a house all day, whilst a white man grinds for you !)

The word "gunyon," or house, they apply to everything that
seems appropriated to contain any article. My husband had a
silver pipe-case for the pocket, and they used to say his pyook
had a "gunyon all along of himself." A dog-kennel would be
" gunyon 'long of dingo," &c.

To make them industrious is utterly hopeless ; nothing but the
present urgent want of anything can induce them to make the
slightest exertion. If a man have one " fig"* of tobacco, and
you promise him another if he will do such or such a service,
you must wait until his stock in hand is exhausted, before there
is a chance of his trying to earn more, though they are always
anxious enough to beg for " Pyook, nyook, owrangey bit o'
bacco" (A pipe, and a knife, and a little bit of tobacco).

A small kind of crayfish frequent the Macquarie, called by
the natives "moramy," and I was desirous of obtaining some,
to see and taste, but nothing short of an exorbitant bribe could
induce the blacks to procure any. They are generally expert
fishermen, and in their methods of capturing their prey, making
snares, and other occupations requiring patience and ingenuity,
they show considerable intelligence and perseverance, despite
their inherent idleness.

The contrivance adopted by a tribe on the Murray river for
catching ducks is particularly clever. They place nets (very
similar to those used by wild-duck trappers at home) over a
narrow portion of the river or " creek" which the ducks frequent,
and then, by chasing and frightening them at a distance, gradually drive the birds near to the snare ; the risk is then that they

* Mr. Meredith tells me that the term " fig of tobacco," so general here, will
not be understood at home, where the same description is not used. That kept
here for general use is " Negrohead," and comes in large kegs, packed closely
in layers of twisted rolls, about eight inches long, and one inch broad ; each
of these being technically termed a " fig." Idle smokers employ their servants to cut it up and rub it, ready for use.

may fly over it; to prevent which, the blacks fling up three-cornered pieces of bark high into the air, at the same time accurately imitating the cry of a hawk, and the poor ducks, stooping to escape the supposed enemy, dart into the snare and are caught.

A very fine and excellent fish is often taken in the Macquarie, called the cod, and though not really a species of cod, greatly resembles that fish in its general shape and appearance, though far more delicious in flavour. The Macquarie cod sometimes weighs seventy pounds or more. The natives catch them with spears made expressly for the purpose, in the use of which they are very adroit. These fishing-spears are twelve or fourteen feet long, made of hard wood, usually some kind of Eucalyptus, well sharpened at the end, but not barbed in any way. The native thus armed crouches or lies down on the overhanging bank of the river, or on a fallen tree or old log over the water, intently and motionlessly watching his prey. He then slowly and stealthily glides his spear down towards the water; then dips it a little way, then pokes it farther and farther, so softly as not to alarm the fish; and when quite certain, with one thrust runs it through the unfortunate cod, and brings him up.

The hunting or war spear is quite a different weapon to this, made of the same kind of wood, but much shorter and thicker, about seven or eight feet long, and barbed for some distance from the point, either by notches cut in the wood, or with sharp fish-bones, or crystals securely bound on with kangaroo sinews. These are most savage-like and fearful weapons, and are thrown to a distance of from seventy to one hundred yards, but rarely with certain effect beyond sixty. A great additional impetus is gained by the manner in which they are thrown. A piece of wood called a "wammara," about two feet long, has a notch or socket made in its upper end, into which the blunt end of the spear is inserted before throwing. The wammara is held in a slanting position with the spear horizontally resting *in* its upper end, and *on* the hand of the spearman, who, in flinging it, suddenly gives the wammara a perpendicular position, and adds greatly to the force of the blow.

The "nullah-nullah" is another fighting weapon, made like

the others, of hard wood, with a round handle widening towards the end into a broad knob, well sharpened on the lower side, like the edge of an axe. They have also formidable clubs, for which I do not know the native name.

The " boomerang " had become familiar, by name at least, in England before I left, although the toys sold in shops as boomerangs are very unlike the real ones, the use of which is extremely curious and ingenious. This weapon consists of a very slightly curved, nearly flat piece of hard wood, about two and a half feet long, and two and a half inches wide; its curve, weight, and the manner in which it is feathered off to catch the wind, being most accurately calculated for it to take the intended direction when thrown, different ones being adapted for different aims. It is never aimed at the object intended to be struck, but thus :— suppose A, B, and C form a triangle; a man at A throws the boomerang towards B, to which point it flies, strikes the ground, and, rebounding, turns towards C, where it strikes (like a good " canon " at billiards). The accuracy with which the natives can hit any object with this singular weapon, and the ingenious invention of it, seem worthy of a higher order of intelligent beings than they are usually considered. I have heard of several persons who have practised throwing the boomerang, but none could succeed so as to bear comparison with a native.

The word " waddie," though commonly applied to the weapons of the New South Wales aborigines, does not with them mean any particular implement, but is the term used to express wood of any kind, or trees. " You maan waddie 'long of fire," means " Go and fetch firewood."

The shields used by the natives are pieces of solid wood about two feet long, something in a long diamond shape, with a loop or handle to hold them by, hollowed from the inner side. These they use with extreme adroitness, fending off blows in every direction, which perhaps may partly account for the non-murderous character of so many fierce encounters among themselves. I have heard some of their white friends confess to having found an hour's " excellent sport " in shying at them cobs of Indian corn, from which the grain had been threshed, but which would still inflict rather a heavy blow; not one of which ever hit the sable target, so nimbly did he ward off every cob with his shield, from his legs just as surely as his head, jumping about and grinning all the time in high glee.

I believe these are all the weapons used by the natives of their own manufacture, and these were formerly all cut and made with sharp flints or crystals; but now those acquainted with Europeans procure more convenient tools. The women make neat baskets and bags of the fine long dry grass common in these colonies (and which I have often thought would make beautifully fine plait for hats or bonnets); they use the currijong bark, too, for the same purpose, and carry about with them in these bags a most strange and useless accumulation of trash. They also sew the skins of kangaroos and opossums together (with sinews for thread, and fish-bones for needles), and fashion these into garments, rugs, or bags. Many of them procure English needles and thread from the settlers, and sew with tolerable neatness.

In the Macquarie, near Bathurst, I first saw the superb green frogs of Australia. The river, at the period of our visit, was for the most part a dry bed, with small pools in the deeper holes, and in these, among the few slimy water-plants and Confervæ, dwelt these gorgeous reptiles. In form and size they resemble a very large common English frog; but their colour is more beautiful than words can describe. I never saw plant or gem of so bright tints. A vivid yellow-green seems the groundwork of the creature's array, and this is daintily pencilled over with other shades, emerald, olive, and blue greens, with a few delicate markings of bright yellow, like an embroidery in threads of gold on shaded velvet. And the creatures sit looking at you from their moist, floating bowers, with their large eyes expressing the most perfect enjoyment, which, if you doubt whilst they sit still, you cannot refuse to believe in when you see them flop into the delicious cool water, and go slowly stretching their long green legs, as they pass along the waving grove of sedgy, feathery plants in the river's bed, and you lose them under a dense mass of gently waving leaves; and to see this, whilst a burning, broiling sun is scorching up your very life, and the glare of the herbless earth dazzles your agonized eyes into blindness, is almost enough to make one willing to forego all the glories of humanity, and be changed into a frog!

In the same pools I found some fresh-water shells, chiefly belonging to the species *Unio, Lymnæa, Stagnalis,* and *Physa,* and, I think, identical with my English specimens. The moramies, or crayfish, live in holes in the muddy banks of these pools; I saw many of their deserted shelly coats, but not any living ones.

That most enigmatical of all the strange animals found in Australia, the Platypus, or *Ornithorhynchus paradoxus,* is also a dweller in the Macquarie, but, being extremely shy, is not often found near Bathurst. So many descriptions have been published of it, that I imagine it is nearly as well understood in England as here. A full-grown specimen is twelve or fourteen inches in length, and much the same shape and proportion as the common mole, with a very thick, soft fur, dark brown on the back, and light coloured beneath; the head and eyes are perfectly *animal,* but in lieu of a mouth or snout, a small flat bill, similar to that of a duck, completes the very odd countenance of this most paradoxical creature. The short furry legs end in half-webbed feet, the hind ones being armed with sharp spurs, which are perforated, and through which, when the animal is annoyed, it is believed to eject a poisonous fluid as it strikes an enemy; but this fact is still doubted by some naturalists, and, like other anomalous peculiarities, is still the subject of argument amongst the learned, to whose information I regret that it is not in my power to add. The creature is very rarely seen on shore, and is usually killed by being shot from a high bank; but this is only practicable when it swims very near the surface.

Among the few living things that frequented the dreary desert plains of Bathurst during my sojourn there, were some flocks of the spur-winged plover; beautiful little birds, whose plaintive cry seemed unceasingly to bewail the dreariness of the spot. It seemed such a miserable place for birds—the gay creatures we love to watch fluttering, and coquetting, and 'sporting about in the green leafy trees—flying in and out—circling and soaring high into the air, then darting back into a thick shady covert, where only the light quivering of the leaves their quick wings fan into motion tells of their hiding-place! Here were neither bush nor tree—nor branches dancing in the sunlight—nor deep clusters of rich dark leaves—nothing but a scorching sky and a desert earth, and the poor plover's sad, melancholy cry, instead of the full, varied choir of airy voices that fills the heart with gladness on a day in spring in green, beautiful old England!

Here and there, amidst the scanty and withered herbage, where the flocks of miserable sheep were vainly trying to pick the fraction of a feed, gleamed up an eye of blue, a bright blue starry flower, looking fearlessly to the fervid sky from its slight and hair-like stem; but its bolder aspect did not prevent my claiming a loving acquaintance with it as a relative of an ancient friend in my own dear land, the harebell. The Australian harebell (*Campanula gracilis*) is scarcely a *bell* at all—rather a star —the corolla being very deeply cleft, and widely expanded; but it is as beautiful: yes, with all my life-long love of the English one, I must acknowledge her antipodean cousin to be even as beautiful as the "poet's harebell," that so merrily dances and waves over British heaths and hills.

In the same barren spots, too, I found a likeness of another old friend, the small meadow convolvulus, the new one being far brighter in hue than the sly, mischievous little sprite that frisks over our English fields, and baffles the sagacity of the neatest farmer when he strives to exclude it. The garb of my new friend is veritable *couleur de rose*, with scarcely a tint of yellow or a gleam of white. The plants were very small and quite compact; the flower growing on a short footstalk, which sprung direct from the root, without any climbing stem. This excessive dwarfishness was probably the consequence of the withering droughts, as in Van Diemen's Land I often gather the same kind in streamers half a yard long, or more; but they usually run along the ground, instead of twining up a bent of grass or any other support.

During our few drives and rambles among the nearest hills, to the north-west of Bathurst, I found some pretty everlastings, *Gnaphalium apiculatum*, and others, with the names of which I am unacquainted. Some of the white ones were large, and grew in handsome clusters, with the soft central florets yellow; looking, at a distance, not unlike the English ox-eye daisy. Others were entirely yellow, and larger than the white ones, growing singly on the stalk, and very handsome, showy flowers, but from their wide open, staring look, always reminded me of those full-blown representations of the sun, so much patronized by country sign-painters. The dry, harsh, juiceless everlastings seemed exactly the kind of growth we might expect to meet in such an arid, parched region as this. They seem as if they could be quite independent of droughts, hot winds, and every other destructive agent of this withering climate, and thrive just as well, or better, on a whirl of dust, than in a shower of rain. I began almost to dislike them for daring to blossom and flaunt in such bright array, when so many fairer and sweeter things were drooping and dying all around. Some of the hills we climbed (having driven across the weary plains to their feet) had really very pretty spots among their little glens and slopes, being well clothed with trees living and growing ; and as green as trees in New South Wales usually are, chiefly consisting of the common acacias, and various kinds of gum, or Eucalyptus, all very much resembling each other, except two species, one of which, the " blue gum," bears large, broad, rather blunt leaves, with a pale blue bloom upon them, which makes a pleasing contrast to the dark olive-green tint of the commoner kinds. The peppermint-tree (*Eucalyptus piperita*) is also a very distinct species, and usually a handsome tree ; I have seen some old ones that an artist would delight to sketch. The bark is often very various in colour, the smooth white portions being overlaid in places with a thin coat partially peeled off, tinted with light and dark grey, red, fawn-colour, and brown of many shades, whilst towards the ground the rough, thicker, more orthodox kind of bark generally remains. The foliage is denser and casts more shade than any other gum-tree ; the leaves are small and very narrow, both sides alike (as are those of the whole family), and thickly, yet lightly grouped on the spray ; their colour also is much brighter and greener than the other kinds, and when in flower, the tree is often a dense mass of blossoms, sweet, luscious-smelling, white-fringed little stars, with myriads of birds fluttering and chirping about them, sucking the honey, and showering down bunches that they pull off in sport and mischief. The scent of the leaves when rubbed, and also their taste, which is very pungent, is exactly similar to that of our English herb peppermint, and I should think an essence might be distilled from them, to serve for the use of both the druggist and confectioner. The leaves are commonly supposed to form the chief food of the opossum both in New South Wales and Van Diemen's Land. These beautiful animals live in hollow trees, and are rarely visible by day, unless, as I have sometimes done, you can see one sitting at his front door (as I suppose we may term the entrance to his habitation), usually a hole far up the tree, whence they descend at night to feed on grass and herbs, and may be seen scampering and playing about like squirrels among the branches. The marks left by their sharp claws in climbing trees are constantly seen, and on the trunks of large old gums tracks of scratches are visible in such numbers as to prove them very favourite places of resort. A full-grown opossum is larger and heavier than a very large cat, with a pretty innocent-looking face, the expression of which is both like that of the deer and the mouse, the shape of the nose and whiskers strongly resembling the latter. The eyes are very dark and brilliant, the ears soft and delicate, the legs short and strong, with monkey-like feet and long sharp claws. They sit up, holding their food in the fore-paws, like a monkey. The tail is eighteen or twenty inches long, about the thickness at the base of a sable boa, and tapering to the end; the under side is quite smooth and devoid of hair, the upper being covered with the same thick woolly fur as the other parts of the body, the colour being either black, dark grey, dark brown, or deep golden brown, like very yellow sable, but always beautifully shaded off from the sides towards the under part, which is lighter. These different colours are most probably also distinctions of species, as no blending or mixture of them is ever observed, which would very likely be the case if they were merely accidental varieties in the same animal, just as we see the common colours of the domestic cat mixed indiscriminately. The tail is strongly prehensile, and holds so tightly, that they often swing their whole weight upon it, and when shot dead, sometimes hang for a minute by it, before falling. Fine moonlight nights often prove fatal to the poor creatures, being the time chosen for shooting them by scores, either for the sake of their warm skins for rugs, or to feed dogs with their luckless bodies. Sometimes they commit sad ravages among the young corn, and then the war waged against them has certainly a fraction more of justice in it; but too often they are, like my poor favourites the Cape pigeons, shot in mere wanton cruelty, which, to gild its villany, assumes the name of " sport." All dogs pursue them to the death, and often in the day-time find one who has either been too idle or unsuspecting to run up his tree, who, unless he can instantly climb one, falls a victim to his imprudence, though not without a most vigorous resistance of sharp bites and scratches, and many a shrill and piercing squeal of agony: as is the general course in this world, either among men or brutes, might is victorious over right, and poor "possey" rarely escapes. The noise they usually make at night, when undisturbed, is something like a very hoarse laugh, a kind of grating throat-chuckle ; and on a still night many of them may be heard calling to and answering each other for a considerable distance.

Like all other animals of their class, they are marsupial, and have rarely more than one young one at a time, which the doe carries about with her, at first in the pouch, and afterwards on her back.

The blacks procure opossums by climbing trees where their holes are, and have evidently some means of ascertaining whether the animal is turned with its head or tail towards them, before touching it ; if the former, they frighten him, or by some means induce him to turn round, when, instantly seizing the tail, they forcibly drag him out. If the hole extends too far for them to reach their prey, they cut a larger hole with an axe or tomahawk.* They often show great brutality in torturing the unfortunate animals they take, long before putting an end to their wretched sufferings. Mr. Meredith on one occasion remonstrated with a black who was cruelly and inhumanly maiming one of these poor harmless creatures, but the only reply the savage made was by a broad grin, and the cool remark, " Bel 'possum cry ! "—(Opossum don't cry !) The natives, like most savages, are very agile in climbing trees, making small notches in the

* Formerly these implements were made of flint or crystal, but now the natives procure English ones.

My omitting all allusion to the kangaroo may be deemed an oversight, but the reason I do not describe them here, is, that I did not see one in New South Wales, nor has Mr. Meredith, in all his wanderings there, met with more than half a dozen. So effectually is the race being exterminated. In Van Diemen's Land they are much more abundant.

bark as they ascend, just large enough to rest the end of the great toe upon, which member seems in them particularly strong, for even in riding on horseback, which many of them do, well and fearlessly, they never put the flat foot in the stirrup, but only lay hold of it with the great toe.

CHAPTER XII.

Emus and native turkeys are not now seen near Bathurst, although still very numerous in the less populous districts. The
bush-turkey is about the same size as a tame one; the colour
dark brown, with light grey feathers on the breast, and full
plumage on the head and neck. They are very shy, and,
being excellent eating, are much sought after by both Europeans and natives. On foot it is all but impossible to approach within gunshot of them, as they take wing on the least
alarm; but they will allow persons on horseback, or in a vehicle
of any kind, to come close to them, and by such means they are
usually taken.

A most extraordinary account is given by Mr. Gould and
other naturalists of the manner in which these birds provide for
the artificial hatching of their young, by scratching together a
great heap of vegetable matter, in which the females lay their
eggs, and leave them, trusting to the heat which the mass ac-
quires during fermentation, to bring out the brood. This, if true
of any Australian bird, is certainly a mistake as regards the
turkey, which frequents the wide, open plains of the interior,
and forms scarcely any nest, but in some accidental hollow lays
several bluish-spotted eggs, which afterwards become much
darker in colour, and are hatched in the usual manner. Were
the birds to form so large and conspicuous a receptacle for their
eggs as I have seen described, namely, a mound of rubbish thirty
feet round, and eight or ten high, none would escape discovery,
and as both eggs and birds are valued as food, the race would ere
this be totally extinct. I never had an opportunity of seeing the

nest of a bush-turkey, and therefore *my* account is but the transcript of what I have been told ; but of my informant's veracity and knowledge I cannot entertain a doubt.

One staple article of consumption, both with emus and turkeys, is the berry of the low-creeping prickly plant called the native cranberry *(Astroloma humifusum)*, which is so very hard that I should think their digestive organs must be akin to those of the ostrich. This semblance of a fruit is about the size of a currant, and with its peach-like bloom looks rather tempting, but a marble covered with thin kid would best represent its flavour and consistence. I remember the shock of disappointment I received on attempting to taste some on a hot thirsty day, and have never since deprived the emus of a single berry. The blossom is very pretty, not unlike a small fuchsia, growing abundantly on the under-side of the trailing sprays, and not often noticeable until a piece is gathered, so closely they lie on the ground.

After a sojourn at Bathurst of about a month, we set forth on our return to Sydney, and the summer being more advanced, and the heat much greater, the weariness and discomfort of the journey were increased tenfold. The mountains were just as dreary as when we crossed them in coming ; the roads not quite so bad, the great holes and reservoirs of mud in them being a little dried up, and the really dry portions rising in continuous volumes of dust.

Equally annoying with the dust was the loud, incessant, and indescribable noise of myriads of large and curious winged insects, commonly and incorrectly called locusts, but which are totally different from any kind of locusts I ever saw either represented in books or in collections. They literally swarm in the summer time on the gum-trees, and are seen flying about in immense numbers ; the noise they make when on the wing being a loud hum or buzz, not nearly so disagreeable as their note when settled on a tree, which most closely resembles the sound of a miniature watchman's rattle ; and when this is multiplied by thousands and millions of these noisy creatures, the din is intolerable. A stocking or lace manufactory is not more distressing to a person unaccustomed to the rattling and riot of the machinery. Whilst we rested one day, a couple of the locusts were caught, and I no longer wondered so much at their loud notes, for they are powerful-looking creatures, something the form of an enormous fly, with stout brown bodies two inches long, six rough legs, a squarely shaped head like a grasshopper's, half an inch or more in breadth, with large prominent black eyes, and a long proboscis, which when at rest lies very compactly under the chin. (I must pray entomologists to forgive my unscientific descriptions, as I am unacquainted with their technical phraseology.) On the front of the head are some jewel-like markings of yellow and red ; the wings are very large, and as transparent as glass, traversed by some very strong and many finer fibres in a beautiful net-work. Altogether they are very handsome and most harmless-looking insects, and I liberated those caught for me, as soon as I had well examined them.

Since leaving New South Wales, I have become rather better acquainted with the locusts, as a species but slightly different inhabits Van Diemen's Land. These are somewhat smaller, with coral-red eyes, instead of black ones, and of a blacker colour generally. They frequent certain kinds of Eucalyptus in countless numbers, but only in particular localities ; we sometimes drive several miles without hearing one, and then suddenly find ourselves in the midst of a whole swarm.

In both Colonies a kind of manna is found upon and lying beneath the trees chosen by the locusts, in snow-white flakes, sometimes soft, and often nearly as hard as a sugar-plum, with a sweet and rather pleasant flavour ; its medicinal properties being the same as those of the manna sold by druggists. Children are very fond of it, but I have never seen it in any quantity.

I have heard very many discussions as to the origin of this manna and its connexion with the locusts, some persons believing that the insects made it, as bees make honey, others that it was a natural exudation from the tree, which attracted the locusts to feed on it. But since I have had opportunities of observing the matter more attentively, I have been convinced that neither of these is the true solution of the mystery, but that the following explanation, given me by our worthy medical attendant here (Van Diemen's Land), Dr. Storey, is the true one.

Beneath the outer bark of some gum-trees is a sweet kind of mucilage, free from the very strong aromatic flavour which per-

vades the rest of the tree; and the locusts, perforating the outer
bark with their long, sharp proboscis, suck out the juice, which
continues to flow for a short time after they leave the aperture,
and drying in the sun, falls to the ground in flakes of manna.
I have had many corroborative proofs of this fact, and, before
knowing it, had often vainly endeavoured to conjecture what
the locusts could be doing, when I saw them covering the
smooth stem of a tree for many yards, and the greater portion of
them motionless.

They evidently pass through one, if not more stages of existence, preparatory to their becoming perfect winged insects. In
the summer, towards evening, it is common to see on the trunks of
trees, reeds, or any upright thing, a heavy-looking, hump-backed,
brown beetle, an inch and a half long, with a scaly coat; clawed,
lobster-like legs, and a somewhat dirty aspect, which is easily
accounted for, when at the foot of the tree a little hole is visible
in the turf, whence he has lately crept. I have sometimes carefully carried these home, and watched with great interest the poor
locust " shuffle off his mortal," or rather earthy coil, and emerge
into a new world. The first symptom is the opening of a small
slit which appears in the back of his coat, between the shoulders,
through which, as it slowly gapes wider, a pale, soft, silky-look-
ing texture is seen below, throbbing and heaving backwards and
forwards. Presently, a fine square head, with two light red eyes,
has disengaged itself, and in process of time (for the transforma-
tion goes on almost imperceptibly) this is followed by the libera-
tion of a portly body and a conclusion; after which the brown
leggings are pulled off like boots, and a pale, cream-coloured,
weak, soft creature very slowly and very tenderly walks away
from his former self, which remains standing entire, like the coat
of mail of a warrior of old, ready to be encased in the cabinets
of the curious; the shelly plates of the eyes that are gone, looking after their lost contents with a sad lack of " speculation " in
them. On the back of the new-born creature lie two small bits
of membrane doubled and crumpled up in a thousand puckers,
like a Limerick glove in a walnut-shell. These begin to unfold
themselves, and gradually spread smoothly out into two large,
beautiful, opal-coloured wings, which by the following morning
have become clearly transparent, whilst the body has acquired

its proper hard consistency and dark colour; and when placed on a gum-tree, the happy thing soon begins its whirring, creaking, chirruping song, which continues, with little intermission, as long as its happy harmless life.

When the locusts happen to come out in the morning, the heat of the sun often dries their unopened wings so suddenly that they cannot expand, and thus, quite helpless, the poor things become a prey to the numerous birds and swarms of ants that are always ready to attack and devour them.

What state the locust passes through previously to its existence as an underground beetle, I am not aware; but in newly-ploughed peat land* great numbers of fat, white, inactive caterpillars or grubs are constantly found, some of which, judging from their size and shape, are probably locusts in their first state of being. I find these grubs some inches below the surface, coiled round in little cells exactly their own shape and size, hollowed in the moist ground, whence they apparently derive their sustenance. When disturbed, they slowly crawl under another piece of earth, where they soon form a new cell, similar to the old one.

Another locust, resembling the one I have described, in every respect except size, is perhaps the male insect, the body being much slighter in proportion, and not exceeding an inch in length. The circumstance of these two sizes in the locusts exactly corresponding with those of two kinds of the ground-grubs, induces me to think that the latter are locusts in their first or lowest form; but my opinions, being formed solely from observation, without that aid which a previous knowledge of entomology would afford me, may very probably be erroneous. The cruelties which all persons learned in that science are perpetually guilty of, and, as it seems, irresistibly tempted to commit, always rendered it abhorrent to me, and consequently I am now nearly if not wholly useless as an observer of my interesting neighbours of the insect kingdom in this populous region; but lest my modest fear of telling what is already known should by any possibility nip some wondrous discovery in the bud, I simply detail my small sums of knowledge, only regretting that the total amount is not greater.

* In Van Diemen's Land.

As we journeyed on, we found it convenient to rest one night at the Rivulet Inn (the scene of such bacchanalian orgies during our up-journey). The inmates were certainly not *so* tipsy, and more of them were visible than before ; but as to *cleanliness*, the word and the meaning seemed equally unknown within, though the paint outside was as bright as ever, reminding one so much of a newly-furbished-up caravan at a country fair, that I almost expected to see a picture of a giant and dwarf in the veranda, or to hear a great drum.   On our retiring for the night (in company with a dark-brown fat candle that smelt most insufferably ill, as it fizzled and flared by turns) to a freshly painted room with very scanty furniture, and a most sombre coloured, hide-the-dirt kind of bed, I instituted an examination into the state of the linen, and believe that half a dozen unwashed chimney-sweeps occupying the same bed for a fortnight could not have left evidences of a darker hue than presented themselves to my horror-stricken eyes.   The blankets corresponded well in colour, but as to exchange those was totally hopeless, we dispensed with their services, and after great difficulty, and most eloquent grumbling from the rum-inspired landlady, I obtained some coarse cotton sheets (linen ones being rarely seen in the Colony), the dampness of which was satisfactory, as it proved they had been acquainted with the wash-tub.

Thrusting the other sable and not inodorous coverings into the farthest corner of the room, I washed my hands, and re-arranged the bed, and had begun to think of sleep, when a loud knocking at the door aroused us—

" Who's there ? "

" If you please, ma'am, Missus wants them sheets you pulled off your bed, for a gentleman as is just come in ! "

With my parasol I poked the things out on the landing, inly congratulating the happy man destined to enjoy such sweet repose ; but I could not help thinking, at the same time, how many pairs of sheets might have been bought with the money the household were drinking at our previous visit ; or even that a white-washed house *with* clean linen would have been preferable to gilding and rainbow paintings without that humble luxury.

The beauty of the vale of Clwydd had become much enhanced

during the interval of our visits by the blossoming of the young gum-trees, and the greater degree of verdure generally perceptible.   I gathered many flowers by the road-side that were quite new to me, including several orchideous plants, and a bright rich blue flower, with gold and black stamens, growing on a straggling branched stem from out a large tuft of tall reedy leaves.   I named it then the "Knight of the Garter," and have often met it since in both Colonies.

Mount Victoria, too, towered above far greener glens and ravines than when we had crossed the pass before ; but once again amidst the forests of those dreary, black Blue Mountains, and all improvement was at an end.   Burned trees, bare ground, and interminable hills once more surrounded us ; the scorching heat of the sun was to me almost overpowering, and, reflected as it was by the dusty, shadeless road into our faces and eyes, became absolutely painful.   Still the time and the journey wore on, and we reached the Weatherboard inn, then wholly at our service, and where an ever memorable luxury awaited us, in the shape of a capacious dish of young potatoes at tea, being the first vegetables we had seen for some time.   Here we also found a clean bed, though the possession thereof seemed a point of dispute with its numerous tenantry ; but this is an almost universal evil in New South Wales, and in wooden houses like the one in question is, I believe, incurable.   A tolerably neat and productive garden adjoined the house, and everything about bore an air of more comfort than the generality of such places in the Colony.

After an early breakfast the following morning, we set forth on foot to visit a waterfall.   Entering a little valley with low hills on either side, we soon reached the borders of a bright brook, that, as it gurgled and glittered over its rocky bed, spoke to me of many a lovely valley and verdant meadow at home, where, instead of being, as here, precious as a fount in the desert, such a stream would be but one among the thousands that gladden the teeming earth.   After our dry and parching journey, it was delightful to walk close beside it—to be quite sure that it *was* water—and when wetted feet did not suffice, to stoop and dabble in it—and scoop it up in tightly-clasped hands to drink— and to step over on its large dry stones, with no very great objection to a splash if one's foot slipped.   All the valley was *green* too,—think of that!   And how exquisitely refreshing such moist greenness was to our dust-blinded eyes!   Tall rushes grew there, and half-immersed water-plants, from amidst which we heard the sonorous " clop, clop " of the great green frogs; and bright dragon-flies darted about among the high waving reeds; and there were gay flowering shrubs with pleasant odours, and the delicate " fringed violet, a gem worthy to grace Titania's rarest crown.   It is an humble lowly flower, about the size of a violet, growing alone on a thin transparent stem some two or three inches high, of a deep bluish lilac rather than purple, and somewhat the shape of the iris, having also the same peculiar lustre, so well described by my poet-friend Mary Howitt—

" As if grains of gold in its petals were set."

The sepals of the flower are edged with the finest fringe, like that which adorns our English bog-bean.   It fades so very soon after being gathered, that I could not even carry one alive to the inn, and never meeting with it again, had no opportunity of sketching it.

As we walked on, a group of slender young gum-trees attracted my attention by their very graceful forms and polished verdure; and when opposite to them, we saw, as through a purposed entrance, that they formed a nearly circular bower, beneath whose leavy canopy dwelt a sisterhood of queens—a group of eight or ten splendid waratahs, straight as arrows—tall, stately, regal flowers, that with their rich and glowing hue,

" Making a sunshine in the shady place,"

seemed like the magic jewels we read of in fairy-tales, that light up caverns by their own intrinsic lustre.

It would have seemed a small sort of sacrilege to disturb this beautiful picture, this temple of the mountain nymphs; so I contented myself with gathering some less fine flowers of the waratah that grew near, and we pursued our way still along the green little valley, and close beside the streamlet, which, as we advanced, flowed much more swiftly, and a sound of pouring water reached us, the cause of which was soon explained by one of the most stupendous scenes I ever beheld, bursting unexpectedly upon us.

Suddenly we found ourselves standing on the brink of a tremendous precipice; for though I have spoken of traversing a *valley*, be it remembered that this was on one of the highest parts of the Blue Mountains, and the valley itself merely a watercourse. I know not how to describe the scene without a comparatively insignificant simile, namely, a theatre, but supposing a space of three or four miles between the centre of the audience-portion and the back of the stage, with a proportionate width. We stood, as it were, in the front of the gallery, which was the summit of a colossal amphitheatre of precipitous and most picturesque cliffs, rising in many places above the point where we stood, and in others broken by rugged ravines, fantastically adorned with trees, that seemed to hold on, like the natives, by a great toe only. At a depth of some hundreds of feet below us lay a thickly wooded undulating vale, a billowy ocean of verdant foliage, stretching far away, and rising again in the distance, until bounded by a towering wall of rocks, their sharp outlines telling in strongly marked light and shade against the clear, deep blue sky.

On our left hand, the bright waters of the mountain stream poured over the rocks in one smooth, glassy, unbroken torrent for some distance, and then, scattered by projecting crags into smaller jets, were lost to view amidst the overhanging trees that fringed the sides of this natural Colosseum.

That portion of the rock near us seemed certainly of an igneous origin, and some more distant parts had much the aspect of basalt, being apparently columnar. Some of the small fragments I picked up had a beautifully crystalline structure, and glittered like " ruby-blende."

I much regretted the impossibility of remaining to have a day or two's exploration about this grand and interesting spot. I should have liked to visit the foot of the cliffs as well as the brow, but this would have incurred a circuit of many miles, and too much fatigue for me to dream of; and with excessive reluctance I retraced my steps to the " Weatherboard," whence we immediately started on our onward journey.

Near the inn we saw some lories, the most brilliant of all the

parrot tribe ; the back and upper portion of the body being a
bright gleaming blue, whilst the breast and under parts are the
most intense rose-colour, or *ponceau*. Gay as were all the parrots
I had previously seen, I gazed on these in sheer wonder, scarcely
believing they could be *real*, as they rose in a flock from the
road before us and flew past, brightening the very sunshine with
their glorious colours.

CHAPTER XIII.

Storm and fine View on Lapstone Hill—Farm-house in the "Public" line—
Arrive at Parramatta—Steamboat—Scenery on the "River"—Sydney—
Christmas-tree—Christmas-day—Tippling Servants.

IN the afternoon we encountered a storm of lightning, thunder,
and rain, just before reaching Lapstone Hill, and whilst we
wound down it we enjoyed as perfect a picture of a landscape
as ever eye beheld.   How I wished, and wished in vain, for some
rare artist to see it with us!—and fancied the versions of its
beauty that Constable, Creswick, Copley Fielding, Cox, or
Turner might give to an admiring world.   I have before endeavoured to describe Lapstone Hill (Chapter VII.): but if
beautiful then, how much more so was it now,—with tall and
graceful gum-trees loaded with their white and honied blossoms,
lifting up their garlanded heads from the deep ravine,—amidst
groups of the delicate, feathery-leaved acacia, whose countless
clusters of pale-golden, hawthorn-scented flowers were bending
with the heavy rain-drops, that glittered and sparkled like diamonds on the shrubs, trees, and deep-crimson waratahs on the
rocks above us!   Before us lay the green Emu Plains, the broad
Nepean, and town of Penrith; the view being bounded on either
side by the rocky gorge through which we looked.   One half of the
sky was black as night, with the yet unspent wrath of the thun-
der-clouds, whose artillery still reverberated grandly amongst the
mountains; the other half of the Janus-faced heaven was blue,
and bright with sunshine: and over both, like a beautiful spirit
of concord, blessing alike the darkness and the light, beamed a
most brilliant rainbow.   The whole scene was so indelibly
painted on my mind, I can fancy now that I see each individual
rock and tree that helped to make up the beautiful whole.

Crossing the Nepean as before, in the punt, we took up our
quarters again at the Ferry Inn, and early the next day continued
our journey.   Seeing a tolerably large house by the roadside,

with stacks, cows, pigs, and other farm-like things about, and a tall sign-post, or what appeared such, in front, we alighted, to see if we could procure a glass of milk, and entered a room, evidently in the " public" line of business, smelling dreadfully of rum and tobacco, and garnished with pipe-ashes, dirty glasses, and empty bottles in abundance. A continuance of loud knocking brought a stupid, dirty, half-dressed, slipshod woman from an inner room, in which, as she left the door open, I could see several messy, unmade beds, soiled clothes all about the floor, and three or four more women of different ages, and of as unpleasing aspect as the one who had obeyed my summons, and who, after some delay, brought me a jug of nice sweet milk, and a dirty glass to pour it into ; seeming to me as if she had ably assisted in the bottle-emptying of the preceding evening. This universal addiction to drink, and the consequent neglect of all industry and decency, are truly shocking. Here was a substantial farm-house (sometimes performing in another character, it is true), with the female inmates half-drunk and scarcely out of bed at ten o'clock on a summer's morning, rooms unswept, beds unmade, and the whole establishment telling of plenty, sloth, and drunkenness.

We reached Parramatta about noon, and remained, in luxurious idleness, at the pretty inn I had so much liked on our previous visit, for a day or two, until lodgings were prepared for us in Sydney. We then embarked in a steamboat named the *Rapid* or the *Velocity*, or some like promising title, on the Parramatta river (*alias* Port Jackson), and moved away from the wharf at a most funereal pace, which I for some time accounted for by supposing that other passengers were expected alongside, but at length found, to my dismay, that it was the best speed with which this renowned vessel could travel without fear of an explosion. One advantage it gave us was a good and deliberate view of the scenery on either side ; a moderately quick draughtsman might have drawn a panorama of it as we slowly puffed along.

Some of the cottages and villas on the banks are very prettily situated, with fine plantations, gardens, and orange-groves around them, and nice pleasure-boats moored beside mossy stone steps leading to the river. As we neared Sydney the banks became

much more rocky and picturesque, skirted and crowned with
pretty native shrubs, with here and there a fantastic group of
crags, like a little fort or castle, perched among them.

The animation of the scene in the harbour, the numerous vessels at anchor, and the busy little boats plying in every direction,
gave by no means unpleasing evidence of our return to the Australian metropolis. Viewed from any point, Sydney cannot fail
to strike a thinking mind with wonder and admiration, as being
the creation of so comparatively brief a space. A large and
well-built town, abounding with all the expensive luxuries of
civilized life—streams of gay equipages and equestrians traversing
the wide and handsome streets—throngs of busy merchants,
whose costly and innumerable goods are being landed from whole
fleets of noble ships that bring hither treasures from all climes—
all this, and more—where, but a few years ago, the lonely native
caught and eat his opossum, or paddled his tiny canoe across the
almost matchless harbour!

Not without strong misgivings as to the equity of such appro-
priations generally, do I make these remarks; but, in the cruel
annals of colonization, I believe that of New South Wales to be
the least objectionable. For the most part it has been peacefully
effected, and the great disproportion of the scanty aboriginal
population to the vast extent of habitable country still
leaves a superfluous abundance to the natives, of both land and
sustenance. Unlike the nobler and far more abused natives of
New Zealand, they attach themselves to no particular spot, but
within a certain wide boundary, which separates them from other
aboriginal tribes, they wander about, without attachment or interest in one portion of country more than another, so that they
can find abundance of food, the vicinity of Europeans' residences
being sought and preferred for that reason.

We now made a few weeks' sojourn in Sydney, which, could
we have laid the dust, moderated the heat, and dismissed the
mosquitoes and their assistants, would have been very pleasant;
but as it was, my colonial enjoyments were limited to our usual
drives, and when able to walk at all, an idle, languid stroll in
the beautiful Government gardens. For some days before Christmas, in our drives near the town, we used to meet numbers of
persons carrying bundles of a beautiful native shrub, to decorate

the houses, in the same manner that we use holly and evergreens at home. Men, women, and children, white, brown, and black, were in the trade ; and sometimes a horse approached, so covered with the bowery load he bore, that only his legs were visible, and led by a man nearly as much hidden ; carts heaped up with the green and blossomed boughs came noddingly along, with children running beside them, decked out with sprays and garlands, laughing and shouting in proper Christmas jollity. I liked to see this attempt at the perpetuation of some of our ancient homely poetry of life, in this new and generally too prosaic Colony, where the cabalistic letters £. *s. d.* and R U M appear too frequently the alphabet of existence. It seemed like a good healthy memory of *home;* and I doubt not the decked-out windows and bouquet-filled chimney in many a tradesman's house gave a more home-like flavour to his beef or turkey, and aided in the remembrance of old days and old friends alike numbered with the past.

The shrub chosen as the Sydney "Christmas" is well worthy of the honour (the rough usage it receives rendering the quality of the post it occupies rather problematical, by the way). It is a handsome verdant shrub, growing from two to twelve or fifteen feet high, with leaves in shape like those of the horse-chestnut, but only two or three inches broad, with a dark green, polished, upper surface, the under one being pale. The flowers, which are irregularly star-shaped, come out in light terminal sprays, their chief peculiarity being, that they completely open whilst quite small, and of a greenish white colour ; they then continue increasing in size, and gradually ripening in tint, becoming first a pearl white, then palest blush, then pink, rose-colour, and crimson : the constant change taking place in them, and the presence of all these hues at one time on a spray of half a dozen flowers, has a singularly pretty appearance. Their scent when freshly gathered is like that of new-mown hay. Great quantities of the shrubs grow in the neighbourhood of Sydney, or I should fear that such wholesale demolition as I witnessed would soon render them rare.

The "Christmas dinner" truly seemed to me a most odd and anomalous affair. Instead of having won a seasonable appetite by a brisk walk over the crisped snow, well muffled in warm winter garments, I had passed the miserable morning, half-dead with heat, on the sofa, attired in the coolest muslin dress I possessed, sipping lemonade or soda-water, and endeavouring to remember all the enviable times when I had touched a lump of ice or grasped a snowball, and vainly watching the still, unruffled curtains of the open window for the first symptom of the afternoon sea-breeze.

I have heard persons who have lived for years in India say that they found the climate of Sydney by far the most oppressive; and I partly account for this by the better adaptation of Indian habitations to the heat, and their various contrivances for relief, which English people, choosing to build English houses in an un-English climate, never dream of providing. The only cool arrangement generally adopted is the substitution of an oiled cloth or matting for a carpet on sitting-room floors; some of the mattings are fine and rather pretty-looking, but the oiled cloth has always a kind of hair-dresser's-shop look about it, which not the most elegant furniture of every other description could reconcile to my old-world prejudices; and the noise which the softest step makes upon it is always unpleasant.

The prevailing vice of drunkenness among the lower orders is perhaps more resolutely practised at this season than any other. I have heard of a Christmas-day party being assembled, and awaiting the announcement of dinner as long as patience would endure; then ringing the bell, but without reply; and on the hostess proceeding to the kitchen, finding every servant either gone out or rendered incapable of moving, the intended feast being meanwhile burned to ashes. Nor is this by any means a rare occurrence; as the crowded police-office can bear ample testimony.

CHAPTER XIV.

Homebush—Colonial Country houses—The "Avenue"—Gates—Slip-rails —Bush-rangers—Mounted Police—Dingoes—Flying Fox—Flying Opos-sum—Native Cats — Birds—Robins—Swallows—Knife-grinder—Coach-man—Bell-bird—Laughing Jackass—Larks—Game.

In January, 1840, we removed to "Homebush," an estate within eleven miles of Sydney, on the Parramatta river, where we proposed residing for a year or two ; and rendered the ill-ar-ranged and dilapidated old house a tolerably comfortable home. It contained two good rooms and five smaller ones ; the veranda in front was one hundred feet long, by twelve in width, and was carried round the ends of the house in the same proportion, the whole neatly flagged ; at the back, the line was broken by the two wings, leaving a shorter veranda in the centre, with the garden (or rather wilderness) before it, commanding a beautiful view of the river (a creek of which ran up towards the house), the oppo-site shores, and several wooded jutting points on our own side.*

Homebush was a fair specimen of a New South Wales settler's residence, possessing many of the Colonial peculiarities. The house stood on the highest ground in the estate, and for some hundreds of acres all around not a native tree nor even a stump was visible, so completely had the land been cleared, although not worth cultivation. This desert bareness was a little relieved close to the house, by three magnificent Norfolk Island pines, which towered far above the roof; and by the then broken and ruined fruit-trees of what had been two very large orchards, which were

* On one of. these was a school for young ladies, and any one addressing the principal by letter would be somewhat amused at the very alarmingly soft nature of the superscription, which would run thus :
"Mrs. Love,
Harmony House,
Concord,
Near Kissing Point ! "

K

formerly well stocked with mulberry, plum, cherry, pear, apple, peach, orange, and loquat trees, but at the time of our taking the place, after its being vacant some years (or only occupied by a drunken overseer), the cattle had free ingress through the broken fences, and the fine orchards were utterly destroyed.

A curving road, nearly half a mile long, and some twenty yards wide, with a good four-rail fence on either side, led from the entrance gate, on the public road, to the house, and this, being unadorned by a single tree, was, according to a Colonial stretch of courtesy, termed the "Avenue ; " much to my mystification, when, on inquiring for Mr. Meredith one day, a servant told me, " Master had just gone down the ' aveny.' " I pondered this announcement some moments, and not being able to recollect any thing of the kind near the place (for I confess my thoughts were wandering in search of some gum-tree likeness of the stately aisles of elms and limes that I loved so well at home), I was compelled to inquire where this " *terra incognita* " lay ; and having once discovered that we *had* an " avenue," I never failed to remember its style and title.

Proceeding, then, along the avenue towards the house, a stranger might be apt to fancy he had entered at a wrong gate, for he would find himself led into the midst of all the farm-buildings ; stock-yards, cow-sheds, barn, stable, and piggeries ranging on his left hand, whilst huts for the farm servants lay on his right ; and in front, commanding a full view of all these ornamental edifices, the hall door of the house ! Such being the almost universal arrangement in the Colony ; and, as compared with many other settlers' houses, this was rather aristocratic. Why the approach to a farm-house here should be so much more dirty, unpleasant, and intrusive than in England, I know not ; but certain it is that in visiting a colonist you are generally obliged to inspect every other portion of the establishment before you can reach the apartments of the family.

Another universal inconvenience is, that you never see a *gate*, or so rarely as only to be the exception to the rule. " Slip-rails" are the substitute ; five or six heavy long poles loosely inserted in sockets made in two upright posts. They may be stepped over by a horse if only lowered at one end, but to allow any vehicle to enter, each one has to be lifted out and put aside ;

and it often happens that four or five of these troublesome and slovenly contrivances occur in the approach to one house, with the invariable additional charm (in winter) of a deep squashy pool of mud around each one; yet, most probably, when you do gain your destination, if a dinner-party be the occasion, you find a table spread with abundance of plate, glass, damask, and costly viands, and a profusion of expensive wines. Such inconsistencies perpetually struck me, showing the general preference for glitter and show, rather than sterling English comfort. A settler will perhaps keep two or three carriages, and furnish his house in a costly style, yet grudge the labour of a carpenter to convert some of the useless wood around him into gates for his farm and grounds. Homebush did possess a gate, but, as was requisite, to be in proper Colonial " keeping," one half was off its hinges, and the companion-moiety never consented to open unless it was lifted; therefore, on the whole, it was remarkably convenient.

During nearly the whole time of our residence here the public road near us was infested by a gang of bush-rangers, or rather footpads, who committed many robberies on persons travelling past; but although we and our servants constantly traversed the dreaded road, we were never molested. Possibly the shelter and concealment they very probably found in some of the dense scrubs and thickets which skirted part of our ground near the scene of their exploits, induced them to adopt the fox's policy, who rarely " robs near his own den;" but the constant depredations we heard of rendered our drives far less pleasant to me, although a double-barrelled gun usually accompanied us. One day we met the clergyman of Cook's River,* who, on his way to dine with the Governor at Parramatta, had been stopped by three of the party, who took his money and a very valuable watch. He had directly ridden to the nearest public-house, not a quarter of a mile off, and, with some of the inmates and an old musket, had diligently scoured the bush in pursuit, but without again seeing the gang, who within an hour robbed some persons in another road. They one day took from a poor woman even her wedding-ring, and for several months continued the same prac-

* Cook's *River* is an arm of the *sea*, running inland from Botany Bay, and on its banks are many pleasant residences, and the prettiest church in the Colony.

tices on this, the most frequented public road near Sydney, almost without an attempt being made for their capture ; for so constantly were they " at work," that had the police been desirous of taking them, they could not have failed. In the case of the more formidable gangs of bush-rangers, who by their outrages often become the terror of a wide rural district, the " mounted police" is an excellent and efficient force. It consists of picked and well-paid volunteers from the regiments in the Colony, and the officers are generally brave and intelligent young men, who, when they *look* for a bush-ranger, generally *find* him ; two terms by no means synonymous among the constabulary.

During our stay at Bathurst, a party of the mounted police went in search of a very daring gang of bush-rangers, or, as they are sometimes called, " bolters." After some search, the officer in command, Lieut. Hilliard (of the 86th or 28th, I forget which), divided his force, taking one route himself, accompanied by a single trooper, and sent the rest in an opposite direction. He had not gone far before he found the gang of seven desperadoes comfortably bivouacking, with eleven stand of arms, loaded, beside them ; and by a sudden and gallant attack, secured them all, and brought them into Bathurst; his prowess being duly appreciated by the settlers, who presented him with a valuable token of their gratitude.

The plan usually pursued by the bush-rangers in robbing a house (which I imagine they very rarely do without collision with the servants) is to walk quietly in, and " bail up," *i. e.* bind with cords, or otherwise secure, the male portion, leaving an armed guard over them, whilst the rest of the gang ransack the house, taking all firearms, money, plate, or valuables, together with what clothes or stores they require. Resistance is out of the question, silence or death being the alternative. One friend of ours on such an occasion sprang across the room to seize his gun, the moment the bush-rangers entered, but they fired, and he was severely wounded, without gaining his object ; another gentleman had several fingers shot off, but the wretches seldom commit murder if their victims quietly submit to their peremptory demands.

Another unpleasant class of neighbours were the native dogs, or dingoes, evidently a species of wolf, or perhaps the connecting link between the wolf and dog. These creatures were very numerous around us, and their howling or yelling at night in the neighbouring forests had a most dismal, unearthly kind of tone. They are more the figure of a Scotch colly, or sheep-dog, than any other I can think of as a comparison, but considerably larger, taller, and more gaunt-looking, with shaggy, wiry hair, and most often of a sandy colour. Their appearance is altogether wolfish, and the expression of the head especially so, nor do their ferocious habits by any means weaken the likeness.

We had a number of calves, which, for greater safety from these savage animals, were folded at night in one of the old orchards adjoining the house; but several of the poor little ones fell victims to the dingoes. Shortly after our arrival at our new residence, we were one night alarmed by a fearful outcry among the calves, and Mr. Meredith, who instantly divined the cause, got up, and found several dingoes dragging along one of the youngest of the herd ; as they ran away he fired, but the night being thickly dark, the brutes escaped. The cries of terror among the poor calves had brought all the cows to the spot, and the indescribable moaning and bellowing they continued until morning showed their instinctive knowledge of the danger. The poor wounded calf was so much injured that it died the following day and its unhappy mother, after watching and comforting it as long as life remained, never ceased her cries and moans till she entirely lost her voice from hoarseness : I have rarely seen anything more distressing than the poor animal's misery ; and to prevent such an occurrence again, the youngest calves were always locked in the stable at night.

The dingoes rarely kill their victim at once, but coolly commence *eating* it, at whatever part they chance to have first laid hold of, three or four often gnawing at the unfortunate animal together, whilst its agonised cries do not seem to disturb their horrible feast in the slightest degree ; and unless by chance a vital part is destroyed, the maimed creature probably lingers during hours of protracted and unimaginable torture.

Their audacity, too, is quite equal to their other engaging qualities. Finding that our veal was not to be obtained, a party of them made an onslaught on our pork, and very early one morning carried off a nice fat pig, nearly full grown. Luckily pigs are not often disposed to be silent martyrs, and the one in question made so resolute a protest against the abduction, that the noise reached Mr. Meredith, who immediately gave chace, and soon met the main body of porkers trotting home at a most unwonted speed, whilst the voice of woe continued its wail in the distance; on coming to the spot, he found two dingoes dragging off the pig by the hind legs towards a thick scrub; he fired, wounding one, when both released their victim and made off, the poor pig trotting home, telling a long and emphatic story of its wrongs and sufferings, from which it eventually recovered. In about two hours after this, a lame white dingo, the same which had been so lately shot at, boldly chased my two pet goats into the veranda!

On one occasion Mr. Meredith was travelling from one station to another with a number of cattle, both old and young, and at night had, as usual, placed them in a secure stock-yard, the calves being with the cows. On going to see them turned out in the morning, the peculiar moaning of a cow struck him as being similar to that of one which had lost her calf; but knowing they were all right the night before, he paid little attention to it, until, on observing a skin and fresh blood just outside the rails, he examined more closely, and found that the dingoes had contrived to drag a young calf through the bars of the stock-yard, and had devoured it (doubtless nearly alive) within a foot or two of the miserable cow, who could see and hear, but not help, her poor little one.

Frequently, when their visits are interrupted, a foal or calf is found with a limb half-eaten away, and the utmost vigilance is requisite to protect the yet more helpless sheep from their ravenous jaws. All flocks are folded at night and watched. Two yards or folds are usually erected near together, between which the watchman has his box, and a large bright fire, and frequently during the night he walks round with his dogs.

I had not the satisfaction of seeing any of the marauders about us taken, though they were continually seen by the servants skulking about, early in the morning, and I have seen them pass through our veranda before sunrise, followed by our own dogs, barking and growling their evident dislike of the intruders. The dingoes do not bark, but howl and yell most dismally. The

Cumberland hounds meet occasionally in the neighbourhood of Homebush, and I hoped they would find and destroy some; but though repeatedly on the scent, they did not succeed, and the members of the "hunt" seemed generally to prefer having their fox (dingo) in a bag, to the trouble, or, as I should have supposed it, sport of finding one in the forest.

The "flying fox" of New South Wales is an animal I do not remember to have seen any published account of, yet it is a very remarkable one. I had often heard Mr. Meredith speak of the quantities of these creatures that he had seen on the shores of the Hunter's River, but was not aware we had any of them near us, until one moonlight night, whilst initiating an English friend into the barbarous mysteries of opossum-shooting (familiarly termed "possumin"), he heard a great flapping and rustling amongst the branches and leaves above his head, and firing, brought down a very fine specimen of the flying fox.

I forget the dimensions which Dr. Buckland assigns to the pterodactyle, the gigantic bat of a former world; but this seemed a not unworthy representative of the species, the wings measuring between four and five feet at their full expansion, and the body being larger than that of a well-conditioned rat. The head more resembles that of a dog than a bat, covered, like the middle and hinder portions of the body, with thick black fur, that round the neck being fox-coloured. The claws and limbs of the wings are very strong, and the membrane very tough and elastic.

These giant bats are especially destructive in orchards, as they have a great penchant for ripe fruit, particularly peaches, and their mode of gathering their dessert not being economical, they knock off great quantities while buffeting about in the trees; added to which, their scent is so exceedingly unpleasant that no fruit they have once touched is eatable.

I never saw any other large bats here. Several of a small kind, apparently very similar to the common little English bat, used to flit about the house in an evening; but I liked them too well to molest them.

One dead specimen of the flying opossum was brought to me. The head greatly resembles in its gentle expression those of the other kinds of opossum, and with a still greater length of prehensile tail. The fore and hind legs on either side are enclosed in the soft, elastic, furry membrane, which spreads like a bat's wing from the back, leaving only the sharply clawed feet exposed. On having the body skinned, I observed that this membrane was double, and easily separated, but without the slightest particle of any other substance between the two thin, almost transparent textures. The upper portion was covered with warm black fur; the under part had a thinner covering of soft, greyish white hair.

Several of the mischievous little animals commonly called native cats (*Dasyurus* ——?) were destroyed by our dogs. They seem to occupy the same place in Australia that the weasel and ferret family do at home, being terribly destructive if they can get into the henhouse; not only killing to eat, but continuing to kill as many fowls or turkeys as they have time for, leaving a sad spectacle of mangled corses behind them. They are pretty, but have a sharp, vicious countenance, very different to the deer-like expression of the herbivorous animals here. Their common colour is grey, finely spotted with white; the tail thin, covered with rather long, wiry hair, which forms a sort of tassel at the end. They are about the size of a lean, half-grown domestic cat, very agile, fierce, and strong, and extremely tenacious of life. Dogs seem to have a natural propensity to destroy them, but sometimes find the engagement rather more equal than they might wish.

Very few birds came near our house, but among those few was the robin (*Petroica phœnicea?*), as much more beautiful in plumage as he is inferior in note to our winter darling in England, but with exactly the same jaunty air, and brisk, quick manner. His attire is, I really think, the most exquisite of all the feathered creatures here: the breast is the most vivid geranium-colour, softening to a paler shade towards the wings, which are glossy black, with clear white markings across them; the back is also black, with a white spot on the crown of the head, and the tail-feathers are also barred with white. The colours are so clear and distinct as almost to convey the idea of different garments put on and fitted with the most exquisite taste; whilst the gay, frolicsome air, and intelligent, bright, black eyes of the little beau tell you that he is by no means unconscious of the very favourable impression his appearance must create. He hops about, sings a few notes of a soft, lively little song; flies to a rail or low tree, and arranges some fancied impropriety in a wing-feather; then surveys the glossy spread of his tail as he peeps over his shoulder, and after a few more hops, and another small warble, very sweet and very low—a passing glance, like the flash of a tiny flambeau, and he is gone!

Some robins, which I supposed the females, have a less vivid scarlet on the breast, though similar in all other respects.

When we first came to Homebush, I observed fragments of many swallows' nests in the veranda, and marks where others had been, but had wholly crumbled away, the constant heat so drying the mud that it could not stick, and the poor birds were in constant danger of losing both their patient labour and their helpless young. To obviate this sad distress, I had a few little shelves nailed up in the most retired part of the veranda, as foundations for the nests, and soon had the satisfaction of seeing a nice strong superstructure raised on one of them, from which in process of time five downy little heads emerged, opening very wide mouths for the food constantly supplied by the parent birds. Only one family placed themselves thus under our immediate protection, but many others built in the old barn and other outhouses.

One bird which frequently came near the house has a very singular note, which has gained for him the Colonial *sobriquet* of the " knife-grinder ;" a portion of his song bearing a most accurate resemblance to the sound of grinding a knife on the grindstone, giving exactly the crrew - - - - whiss - ss - ss -, but in a most musical and dulcet tone. His attire, as befitting an artisan, is somewhat sober and plain.

Another equally singular voice among our feathered friends was that of the " coachman," than which no title could be more appropriate, his chief note being a long clear whistle, with a smart crack of the whip to finish with. Although I have often heard his fine clear voice sounding far above me, from his favourite perch in the top of the highest tree near, I never had a distinct view of Mr. Jehu.

The " bell-bird " has, as may be supposed, won its appellation from the resemblance of its deep full voice to the tones of a bell; and that general favourite, the " laughing jackass," equally well merits the first portion of his title, by his merry and most musical peals of laughter; but why he should be called a "*jackass*" at all, I am at a loss to divine. Under this name, however, he is generally respected in the colony, being an adroit destroyer of snakes, guanas, and other reptiles. When many of these merry birds congregate together, the effect is extremely droll: first one begins alone, and laughs lustily out at the top of his voice; a second, third, and fourth then take up the strain, like glee-singers, till the whole party are fairly off, and the very trees seem to peal out along with them. I am half inclined to fancy that Martini's popular laughing chorus, " *Vadasi via di qua*," must have been suggested by the voices of my friends the Australian jackasses; certain it is, that both songs have an equally infectious spirit, and set the most gloomy-minded listener laughing in concert, whether he will or no. The poor birds often fall victims to their own accomplishments, for, being much esteemed as " pets," they are frequently maimed to prevent their escape, and tied by the leg or closely caged, whilst their less human persecutors spoil their naturally merry voices by teaching them a few lame bars of some London-alley tune ; and " All round my Hat," " Jump Jim Crow," or " Sich a getting up Stairs," tells a melancholy story of their miserable fate.

Many small birds, with which I am not sufficiently acquainted to describe them, inhabited our woods ; and one or two kinds of " larks," as they are called, used to rise in considerable numbers from the dry grass-tufts, as we walked over the cleared land. A few quail, a chance wild duck or teal, and one solitary snipe, formed our list of game at Homebush, and I scarcely saw a parrot during our stay.

CHAPTER XV.

Norfolk Island Pine—English Pear-tree—Daisy—Bush Flowers—Creepers
—" He-oak"—Zamia—" Wooden Pear-tree"—Native Cherry—Insect Ar-
chitecture—Twig Nests, &c.—Butterflies—Ground-Spiders—Tarantula—
Silk-Spiders—Scorpions—Hornets—Mosquitoes—Ants.

THE Norfolk Island pine (*Aracauria excelsa*), of which, as I
have before remarked, we had three magnificent specimens close
to the house, is certainly the most noble and stately tree of all
the pine family that I have ever seen, beautiful as are they all.
The tall, erect, and tapering stem (seventy or eighty feet high),
the regularity of the circling branches, lessening by small degrees
from the widely-spread expanse below, to the tiny cross that
crowns the summit of the exquisite natural spire, and the richly
verdant, dense, massive foliage clothing the whole with an un-
fading array of scale-armour, form altogether the finest model of
a pine that can be imagined. The cones too are worthy to
grow on such a tree; solid ponderous things, as large as a
child's head—not a *baby's* head, neither—with a fine embossed
coat of mail, firmly seated on the beam-like branches, as if defy-
ing the winds to shake them.

Mr. Meredith climbed very nearly to the summit of our tallest
pine, and said he had never seen anything more beautiful than
the downward view into and over the mass of diverging branches
spread forth beneath him. He brought me down one cone, with
its spray, if so I may call the armful of thick green shoots that
surrounded it, and I was gazing at it for half the day after; it
was so different from anything I had seen before, so new, and so
grandly beautiful. The rigidity of the foliage had a sculpture-
like character, that made me think how exquisitely Gibbons
would have wrought its image in some of his graceful and stately
designs, had he ever seen the glorious tree.

One of those at Homebush grew near to the front veranda,

and some of its enormous roots had spread under the heavy stone pavement, lifting it up in an arch, like a bridge.

When the cones ripened, the large winged seeds fell out in great numbers; they require to be planted immediately, if at all, as the oil in them quickly dries out, and with it the vegetative properties are lost.

Close under the towering pines grew a common English pear-tree; a crooked, wide-spreading, leafy, farm-house-garden sort of pear-tree, that won my especial love, from the good old-fashioned pictures of gable-ended houses and neat garden-orchards it brought into my mind, and the glory and delight of its spring-time blossoms was an earnest and most child-like joy to me. Surely never was pear-tree so watched and gazed on, both morning, evening, and moonlight!—for Sydney moonlights are like tropical ones, so clear, so silver-bright, that I could see to read small print as well as by day—and the old pear-tree shone out in them like a beautiful vision of home, telling store of pleasant stories in each fluttering leaf that fell from its thousands of flowers—telling of bloomy fragrant gardens, with velvet turf paths, and shady arbours, and singing birds, and little running brooks, *one* of whose silver threads near our thirsty home would have been a priceless treasure—oh! it was an exhaustless remembrancer of pleasant by-gones was that old pear-tree!

Its rival in my home-loving regards was a little root of the double daisy, which, as a great treasure, my husband brought me one day from a gardener's. It lived, as very few daisies do at home, I can tell them, in a pot by itself, and was carried into the shade, and watered daily, and tended with as much solicitude as any *rara avis* of the choicest conservatory. It bore two nice pinky-white daisies, just like real English ones; and then, during an illness I had, in which I could not attend to it, it withered away, and my first glance into the garden showed me the scorched remains of my poor favourite.

Many very pretty native flowers and shrubs adorned our "bush," or rather forest, and the graceful native indigo crept up many bushes and fences, sometimes totally hiding them with its elegant draperies. Another handsome climber of the same family (*Kennedia*) has rich crimson flowers, very long in the part called the keel, with bright yellow stamens protruding from its point.   This species climbs to a height of twenty or thirty feet, and the dark leaves and drooping flowers hang down in elegant pendulous wreaths.   But the most beautiful climbing plant I have yet seen in Australia, I know not the name of, nor can I find any botanical description to suit it, except that of *Bignonia Australis,* which it possibly is.   The leaves resemble those of the jessamine in form, but are much larger, and of a rich glossy green ; the flowers fox-glove shaped, in long axillary sprays, their colour being a delicate cream-colour, beautifully variegated within by bright purple markings.   I only found one plant of it, in a (comparatively) cool moist thicket in our Homebush wood.

Great quantities of a tall, handsome, herbaceous plant, commonly called the "mock-cotton tree," grew near us, and by the roadsides around Sydney, it having at one time been introduced as a probably profitable speculation, but the cotton was not found to be a marketable article.   The clusters of white flowers are extremely beautiful, having very much the structure of the *Hoya carnosa,* and are full of clear honey.   I used to put them to a very ignoble use, namely, as fly-cages, to attract the troublesome swarms from our picture-frames, which the honey-laden blossoms effected to a great extent.

The seed-pods are large, and full of most beautiful soft filaments, like white floss silk, which before they are ruffled by the wind have a bright and silvery gloss, that might well tempt a trial of so fair a material in manufactures.   It looks as if it might be spun into an exquisite stuff between cambric and satin ; and I think still, that some clever genius of the spinning-jennies might weave us a most dainty and gossamer fabric of its fine and even threads, which are the wings of the seeds, and being so light and long, waft them an immense distance, often to the annoyance of the agriculturist, who would by no means partake in my idle admiration of his insidious foe.   I suppose it is a species of *Asclepias.*

Small shrubs with yellow and orange papilionaceous blossoms abounded everywhere, some clinging to the ground like mosses, and others, with every variety of soft and hard, smooth and prickly leaves that can be imagined, growing into tall shrubs, all very pretty, but with so strong a family likeness that I grew fastidious among them, and rarely gathered more than two or

three.   A small scentless violet and a bright little yellow sorrel
(which is an excellent salad-herb) made some few patches of the
dry earth gay with their blue and golden blossoms, and the ground
convolvulus and southern harebell seldom failed to greet me in
our rambles.   Various kinds of epacris also abounded, with delicate wax-like pink and white flowers.

The trees called by the Colonists " he-oak" and " she-oak" (*Casuarina stricta* and *C. torulosa*) form a remarkable feature in
Australian scenery.   They are usually of rather handsome forms,
with dark, rough, permanent bark, and brownish-olive foliage, resembling in structure the " horse-tails" of English brooks, consisting of long tufts of jointed grassy branchlets, hanging down
like coarse hair, or a horse's tail.   The he-oak has much shorter
tresses than the she-oak, which may perhaps have given rise to
the absurd Colonial distinction of the species (as they belong to
the order *Monœcia*).   The blossoms in spring appear like a small
crimson fringe on portions of the branches, and the succeeding
cones are the size of a pigeon's egg, very roughly tubercled.
Perhaps none of all the novel trees in this Colony have so completely strange and un-English an aspect as these ; and in a
moderate breeze the tones uttered amongst their thousands of
waving, whispering strings are far from unmusical, and reminded
me of the lower, wailing notes of an Æolian harp.   However
luxuriant may be the foliage of one of these singular trees, the
skeleton form of the branches is never hidden, but every twig
shows itself, making a drawing of one rather a puzzling affair to
so humble a limner as myself.

She-oak is especially liked as fuel.   It is said that this name
has been borrowed from the *sheac*, or cheoak, of America, in consequence of some resemblance in the wood.

The zamia, now so well known in English stoves, I have often
observed near Sydney, with its handsome coronet of palm-like
leaves gracefully spreading round the central cone.   Near the
road to Cook's River they grow very numerously.

The name, and some resemblance in form between the seed-
vessel and the fruit, form all the likeness which the famed
" wooden pear-tree" of Australia bears to its more useful namesake at home.   One or two large specimens of the wooden fruit
which I saw were the size of a good Jargonelle pear.   When

ripe, they split open from end to end, showing a solid wooden structure, with the thin winged seeds scaling off the inner sides. Several other shrubs bear similar seed-vessels of a smaller size. The "native cherry" (*Exocarpus cupressiformis*) has no better claim to its borrowed title than the pear-tree, being in foliage more like a cypress, but of a brighter and yellower green than the generality of trees in this ever-brown region. Its form is usually handsome, although it seldom attains a large size, and the wood is remarkably close, hard, and finely grained, well adapted for turning or carving. The fruit, so celebrated among Antipodean contrarieties for having the " stone outside," is like a small yew-berry, but still less pleasant in flavour, with a hard seed growing from its end, fancifully termed the stone. Of all countries or climates, I think that of Australia must be the most barren of useful natural products of the vegetable kingdom ; for this miserable " cherry" is the best specimen of its indigenous fruits, if not the only one; nor am I aware of any one edible grain or root fit for human food. Some florid descriptive writers have, I know, luxuriated in depicting imaginary gardens of "parsley and wild carrots," amidst which the cattle are said to revel in abundance ; but whilst in the Colony I never heard of such things. Perhaps the wretched root which, as I have before mentioned, the aborigines dig for when all other sustenance fails them, may be the "carrot" in question ; but it is too hot, stringy, bitter, and small to be of the slightest use to Europeans.

Some of the insect-architects here are most extraordinary creatures ; but I grieve to say I know comparatively little about them, my chief acquaintance being with their deserted houses, of which I have several kinds. Some of these are formed of straight twigs, the sixth or eighth part of an inch thick, and from two to four inches long, placed side by side in a circular form, and very strongly webbed together within, so that it is impossible to tear them asunder without breaking the twigs, the ends of which usually project beyond the closed portion of the cell, which is suspended by a strong web woven over the spray of a tree or shrub, so as to let it swing with the wind. I have sometimes seen a large white caterpillar inside an unfinished cell, and on one or two occasions have observed a bush or tree so full

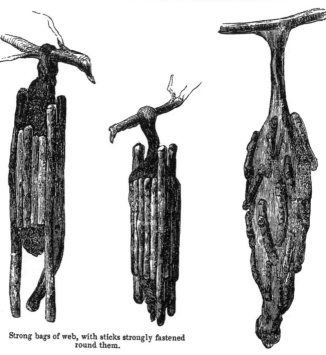

Strong bags of web, with sticks strongly fastened
round them.

Bag of silky web, with small twigs
woven and cemented on it.

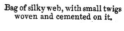

Cone of web, with dry leaves
loosely attached to it.

Cone of web, with small twigs
and grass straws attached.

Cell like an egg, stuck on a twig.

of these pendent berths as to give them the appearance of a good crop of some fruit or seed ; but (very stupidly) I always limited my collection to the vacant ones, or I might have learned much more of their economy.   How such a creature could cut off, and carry to their destined place, pieces of twig four or five times its own weight, I cannot imagine : that they were cut expressly for the purpose is evident from the neat manner in which the ends are rounded off : they are left of uneven lengths, and not webbed on the outside, which, together with their being hung so as to wave with the leaves of the tree, seem all precautions against discovery.

Some are formed in the same manner of much smaller twigs ; others are pointed bags of strong web, with small bits of stick fastened at intervals on the outside ; and some are formed of a webbed bag, to which quantities of small dead leaves are attached by one end only, so as to cover it entirely, and flutter like a withered bunch of leaves ; but all are hung upon trees as much resembling the nests in colour and aspect as possible.   Those I have opened are lined within with the smoothest white silken web, the outer portion being brown or ash-coloured, to correspond with the tint of the twigs or leaves.

I have two examples of another kind of cell, like a very small bird's egg, of a brown ash-colour, with one end open and the other firmly attached to a twig.   At first it might be mistaken for the empty seed-vessel of a plant (had I not gathered it from a pod-bearing shrub) ; but on inspection the cell seems evidently built upon, not grown out of, the spray.   The egg-shape is perfect, and the open end smoothly finished.   Both those I found were empty, their texture was quite smooth and hard, the same substance to all appearance as the bark on which they were so firmly lodged.

I saw very few butterflies in New South Wales, not more than two species, I think, both of a finely spotted copper colour. Large moths are more numerous ; but of these I did not notice many remarkable ones.   Whilst we were at Bathurst, the settlers were complaining of a kind of white grub which infested the roots of the corn, and by eating through the stalks destroyed the crops ; I have seen half a dozen, or more of them, at one root. Before we left Bathurst, a prodigious number of small copper

L

butterflies were seen flying about, and I had strong suspicions of their being identical with the destructive grubs.

The ground-spiders may well be ranked among the wonderful native architects of Australia; they are of various sizes, and differ in their colour, form, and markings. They hollow a circular hole in the earth, adapted to the size of their body, and more beautifully formed and perfectly round than any engineer with all his scientific instruments could have made it. Within, it is nicely tapestried with the finest web, woven closely over the wall of this subterranean withdrawing-room, the depth of which I never accurately ascertained, as at a certain distance they seem to curve, or perhaps lead into a side-cell, where the feelers of fine grass I have introduced could not penetrate. Some of these tunnels terminate at the surface with merely a slight web spun over the grains of soil close to the aperture, as if to prevent their rolling into it; the holes being from one-sixth of an inch to an inch or more in diameter. Some of them boast the extraordinary luxury of a front door; these I imagine to be rather first-rate kind of spiders, and their doors are as beautiful instances of insect skill and artifice as any that our wonder-teeming world displays to us. When shut down over the hole, nothing but the most accurate previous knowledge could induce any person to fancy they could perceive any difference in the surface of the soil; but, perhaps, if you remain very still for some minutes, the clever inhabitant will come forth, when you first perceive a circle of earth, perhaps the size of a wedding-ring or larger, lifted up from beneath, like a trap-door: it falls back gently on its hinge side, and a fine, hairy, beautifully pencilled brown or grey spider pops out, and most probably pops in again, to sit just beneath the opening, and wait for his dinner of flies or other eatable intruders. Then we see that the under side and the rim of his earthen door are thickly and neatly webbed over, so that not a grain of soil can fall away from its thickness, which is usually about the eighth or tenth of an inch, and although so skilfully webbed below, the upper surface preserves exactly the same appearance as the surrounding soil. The hinge consists also of web, neatly attached to that of the lid and the box. I have the greatest respect and admiration for these clever mechanics, and though I very often, with a bent of grass or a soft green twig, try to persuade one to come up and be looked at (which they generally do, nipping fast hold of the intrusive probe), I never was guilty of hurting one. I have picked very large ones off ground that the plough had just turned over, and have carried them to places unlikely to be disturbed: and I generally have two or three particular friends among them, whom I frequently take a peep at. They often travel some distance from home, probably in search of food, as I have overtaken and watched them returning, when they seldom turn aside from hand or foot placed in their way, but go steadily on at a good swift pace, and, after dropping into their hole, put forth a claw, and hook the door to after them, just as a man would close a trap-door above him when descending a ladder.

The tarantula is not quite so great a favourite with me, as I have strong suspicions of its bite being venomous. At first I understood them to be harmless, although servants and ignorant people hold them in great abhorrence, and, unless too frightened to approach, always kill them when discovered. Certainly the appearance of a full-sized tarantula is by no means prepossessing. An oval body nearly an inch long, and a proportionably large head and shoulders, are surrounded by eight bent-up legs, two or three inches long, covered, as are also the head and body, with thick, fine, brown, hair-like fur. When disturbed they scramble along at a rapid rate, and are very frequent residents behind pictures or furniture against the wall, often causing terrific screams from one's housemaid, which are somewhat alarming, until, on inquiry, the dreadful words " A *Triantelope*, Ma'am !" are gasped out, and the tragedy ends in the death, or, as I usually arrange it, the careful expulsion of the intruder.

Not being learned in entomology, I know not if the tarantula is a spinning spider or not, but I never saw one in a web, or detected any thread attached to their bodies. Out of doors their favourite haunts are old trees, where they live between the loose bark and the wood, or in cracks of wooden fences ; and from the large families of several generations which I have sometimes discovered, I imagine their habits to be somewhat patriarchal.

Several persons of education and intelligence have assured me of their dangerous nature, but I have never yet witnessed an instance of it, and they are such patient and industrious flycatchers, that so long as they confine their perambulations to the ceiling, or the upper portion of the walls of a room, I never disturb them.

Many other large kinds of spider are common, and frequently in the woods I have found some with immense webs of dark yellow silk, which would bear a tolerable pull without breaking; the threads being far thicker and stronger than those of the silkworm, and often stretched from tree to tree in a length of several yards. The weavers of these are very handsomely marked spiders of various colours, bright green being a prevalent one. If, as I remember hearing some years since, spiders' web can be spun into gloves and lace, the manufacturers would do well to procure a supply of the raw material from Australia.

We once found what appeared to be the first essay of a numerous family of young spiders at setting up in life on their own account. The large parent web, of strong bright silk, was spread out in all its exquisite and regular divisions across a path, with the portly owner daintily arrayed in green, with leopard-spot markings, staidly poised in the centre; and close by, scattered amongst the twigs and leaves of the thick shrubs, hung a multitude of *little* starry webs, with a little spider seated in the midst of each, all exactly the same size, and bearing a strong filial resemblance to the large one.

The scorpion is a far more truly formidable creature than the tarantula, and, as it frequently lives in old wood, is apt to be brought into the house with the fuel. It is the real, orthodox, zodiacal scorpion, with its hideous scaly, claw-armed body, and long jointed tail, ending in a fearful sting, a wound from which is severely painful, and often of dangerous consequence. It is, without doubt, the most horrible-looking of all the creeping and crawling fraternity that I am acquainted with; and even my philanthropy cannot defend the detestable scorpion, which I ruthlessly kill whenever an opportunity offers. Those I have seen in these Colonies are about two inches long, the tail being about half the entire length; and when the creature is disturbed, this diabolical tail seems to turn on a dozen pivots, darting in every direction, until, when hard pressed or wounded, the creature most assuredly stings itself (even without being " girt by fire"), but whether accidentally, or with intent to commit *felo de se*, of course no one can decide, unless some vicious, venomous individual who *was* a scorpion " in Pythagoras' time" can throw light on this poesy-honoured question! On several evenings I was driven from the veranda, where we commonly sat for some time after sunset, by the sudden appearance of great numbers of large hornets flying in all directions; and the cattle and horses seemed, by their half frantic demeanour and loud cries, as well aware as ourselves what dangerous visitors had arrived, although we did not find that any of the animals were stung. All the fences near the house were thickly occupied by the hornets, who seemed, by their loud buzzing and rapid movements, to be themselves in a state of great excitement. These tumultuous and most unpleasant assemblies took place for several evenings in succession, but fortunately the terror of all our household sufficed to keep every one as much within doors as possible, and we all escaped being stung. I did not even see a single hornet in the house, which, with such countless swarms careering through the air all around, and even in the veranda, seems rather singular.

Mosquitoes used to rise in positive clouds from the banks of the creek in the evening, and if I dared to remain then near the water, they severely punished my temerity, their long sharp proboscis piercing like a fine needle through shoes, gloves, dress, or shawl, and the shrill hum of some hundreds round my face seeming to promise a still further increase of their delicate attentions. A precipitate retreat was my only resource, for most fortunately we were rarely annoyed by them within doors, and there at least I could escape the torments.

But the house, as if no place in this Colony could be free from nuisances, was assailed by myriads of ants, that made their way into every description of sweet stuff, through every kind of barrier; jars, canisters, boxes, and papers were alike unavailing; whatever I touched seemed alive with ants, and their industry was unwearied; day and night the "runs," or paths they traversed, were always black with their countless millions, like a miniature Cheapside or Ludgate Hill, and none of our destructive or protective measures seemed to make the least difference. If one million were scalded, two more supplied their place, and I have met some of the little foragers with bits of sugar in their mouths far down the garden, showing their plans of business to be on a most extensive scale.

CHAPTER XVI.

Guanas—Lizards—Snakes—Salt - Marshes—Fishing—Crabs —'Toad - fish—
Mangrove-trees—Romance and Reality—Night Sounds—Orange-groves—
Gardens—Gigantic Lily—Scarcity of Fresh Water—Winter Rains—Salt
Well—Climate in Winter—Society—Conversation—Servants—Embark
for Van Diemen's Land.

MANY large kinds of guanas inhabit New South Wales; some,
which have been described to me, must be enormous reptiles. I
have only seen two species, the most common being generally
called the sleeping lizard, and is found also in Van Diemen's
Land. It is about a foot or fourteen inches in length, the body
dark coloured, fat, and bloated-looking, the tail short and thick;
the head broad, with a snaky expression, and a long blue tongue,
which gives the poor animal a terrible reputation among the
vulgar, who declare that so blue a tongue must be a proof of its
venomous nature. I believe, if the poor stupid creatures had
the sense to keep their ill-hued tongues out of sight, many hundreds would escape violent deaths. Contrary to the habits of
most lizards, which are remarkable for their extreme activity and
timid alertness on the approach of a footstep, or the slightest
noise, the sleeping guana is often seen lying in the midst of the
road, and frequently the crushed body of one bears disastrous
evidence of the fatal consequences of indolence. Sometimes we
have turned aside to avoid driving over them, or have bestowed
a light lash of the whip in passing, which only caused them to
crawl slowly away, as if our friendly hint were a most officious
and impertinent proceeding, and they had rather a preference for
being trodden or rolled to death. They are most undeniably
ugly creatures, although without the hideous pouch-cheeks of
the West Indian guanas; but we always considered them quite
harmless, until a little incident which occurred since our residence in Van Diemen's Land led us to suspect them of being at

least capable of mischief. One day, last summer, we found one lying in our path, during a bush-ramble; and without any intention to hurt or annoy the animal, but merely to intimate that its place of repose was an unsafe one, Mr. Meredith touched it gently with the barrel of his gun, when, instead of retreating as might be expected, it turned fiercely round, and snapped repeatedly at the gun, just as a savage dog would do, and bit so sharply and strongly as to cut into the solid iron with its teeth, as deeply as a hard stroke of a diamond cuts into glass. Had a hand or foot been in the place of the gun, a fearful wound must have been inflicted. Still, as they appear only to act on the defensive, I see no reason for wantonly destroying them, although I would not advise any·one to incur their bite.

My other acquaintance in the guana family is a far less loathsome creature; I have only seen one specimen, which Mr. Meredith shot, as it was swiftly climbing a tree, with only its head exposed, watching his movements. The head and body of this together were not more than ten inches long, but the slender tapering tail measured more than twice as much. The head had no pouch-cheeks, but was a sharp, knowing-looking lizard's head, covered with small, close, hard scales, as were the entire body, tail, and legs; the feet had long toes, and long, sharp, black claws, evidently well adapted for climbing trees, and seeming as if, like the natives' yahoo, it could turn its feet any way required. The whole of the creature was most beautifully piebald black and white, and in some parts the old scaly coat was shelling off, leaving a brighter new one below. This guana had moveable teeth, like those of the snake, but, I need scarcely say, we were not anxious to experimentalize upon their qualities. By the ignorant, and even by some persons who might be supposed to know better, these animals are termed goannas, and I have heard of a " great pianna " among them.

Numbers of a small kind of lizard, about five or six inches long, used to frequent the garden as well as the " bush," and two took up their abode in my china-pantry, where I often saw them crouching motionless on the dresser, watching the flies till one came near enough to be snapped up in their nimble jaws. Flies were so great a torment, that I respected anything which aided to destroy them, and accordingly never molested the lizards;

but my housemaid, who, I fear, was destitute of all taste for
natural history, had a great dread of my poor friends, and either
used to run shrieking away, or fling something at them whenever they ventured into her sight. They were agile, delicate
little creatures, with bright black eyes, slender long-tailed bodies
of a mottled grey and pale brown colour, and extremely fine
small feet and toes. Still, they were reptiles, and the common
prejudice against their race extended even to these very harmless
little creatures.

With the snake tribe in New South Wales, I am happy to say
my personal acquaintance is very limited, for I fully partake in
the horror usually and very reasonably entertained of them.
Our servants had frequently raised an alarm about a " large black
snake," which lived in an unoccupied hut near the house, but it
always vanished before a gun could be brought, and we rather
discredited the story, until on one occasion the alarm being, I
suppose, more quietly given, Mr. Meredith succeeded in shooting
it through the head, to the extreme satisfaction of the whole
household. It was not a large snake, not being more than four
feet long, of a purplish black colour, with a kind of damson-
bloom on the skin, instead of a polished appearance, which most
of them have, and down each side was a streak of dim red. The
extreme tenacity of life in these reptiles, or more probably the
long continuance of muscular power and motion, even after the
head has been wholly severed from the body, has given rise to a
common idea that at whatever time of the day a snake may be
killed, it cannot *die* until sunset. The extraordinary activity
with which the tail-end of the creature will leap and jump about,
whilst the head is swiftly travelling in another direction, is
horrible to see; it seems as if every joint had a vitality of its
own, entirely independent of brains, or spinal cords, or any other
imagined seat of life.

One of our men-servants told a story of a large black snake
which lived in his hut a long time, and used to lie on his bed at
night, until he took unto himself a wife, who, very naturally,
demurred at the presence of so suspicious a bed-fellow, and induced him to kill it. The large kind called the diamond snake
is (for a snake) as handsome a creature as can be conceived,
being most exquisitely adorned with various colours, like mosaic-

work. Could a lapidary imitate its varied markings in a girdle or bracelet of gems and gold, his fortune would be made.

During our walks in the forest we frequently saw a smaller kind of snake, about two feet long, and so exactly similar in colour to the dead sticks and leaves with which the ground was covered, as not to be observed until they moved: I several times have most narrowly escaped treading on them, which, as all the snakes known in this Colony are venomous, would be a dangerous accident. Some species are far more fatal than others, and of a few the bite is certainly mortal. Among the latter, the small one commonly called the whip-snake, or death-adder, is the most rapidly fatal of all. Several instances of immediate death from its bite were related to me. On the victims in two cases, my informant, our friend Mr. Dunn, of the Hunter River, had, as coroner for the district, held inquests; the evidence proving that in one instance death ensued in seven minutes after the bite, and in the other in eight, the sufferers being scarcely conscious of having been hurt, so very slight had been the puncture, and so wonderfully subtle the poison. It may well be imagined that these dreadful occurrences did not tend to diminish my terror of snakes.

One portion of our land at Homebush consisted of salt-water marshes, covered in high tides, and producing immense quantities of a species of samphire. Through these marshes deep drains had been cut and embankments formed, evidently at an enormous expenditure of labour, but for what purpose we never could divine. One of these drains, which, being very old, had become quite natural-looking, with shrubs, trees, and all kinds of growth adorning the banks, had a sort of wide flood-gate next the creek, through which the tide flowed and ebbed, bringing with it quantities of fine fish, bream and mullet especially. A couple of narrow logs formed something of an " Al Sirat " across the deep channel, which was about twenty feet wide, and on this crazy bridge Mr. Meredith used to station himself to fish; but not being a votary of the (so *called* " gentle craft" of quaint old Izaak Walton, he found a spear armed with a strong barb a more efficient weapon than the rod, and often caught some very fine fish. I, meanwhile, read, sketched, or more frequently idled away an hour or two in watching the myriads of small crabs with which the muddy banks were thickly peopled. At a certain state of the tide they might be seen scrambling out of the water by thousands, and often reminded me of a hungry cargo of stage-coach passengers, to whose dinner only a limited time can be allotted; for the whole troop, after sidling a short distance from the water, immediately commenced eating most expeditiously, picking up some mysterious comestible from the soft rich mud, first with one claw and then with the other, and continually carrying the supplies to the mouth, which, being situated in the broad central region, always gave the idea of a person very busily engaged in filling his waistcoat-pockets; and the effect of some thousands of these odd little bodies all engaged in the same manœuvres was droll in the extreme. If disturbed, they instantly began turning round and round on one claw, as it seemed in a kind of *pirouette*, using themselves as an auger to work their way down, and in an incredibly short time were all lost to view. Occasionally, two happened to fix on the same spot to bore into, or probably old holes remained in the mud, only slightly hidden by the last tide, and access to the known sanctuary was disputed ; in this case there was usually a great deal of clawing and turning under and over, which ended in the combatants both waltzing away together under the mud. These crabs were of various colours, some red, others black, and some dark green. On the sandy beaches near Sydney I have seen some very small ones, of a fine blue, just as busy pirouetting into the white sand as my Homebush friends were in the black mud. The larger ones had bodies the breadth of a dollar, whilst some of the small were not bigger than a fourpenny-piece.

A disgusting tenant of most of the shores around Sydney, and of ours in particular, is the toad-fish: most admirably named : it looks precisely like a toad elongated into a fish, with a tough, leathery, scaleless skin, and a bloated body, dark mottled brown above and white beneath. It is usually about five inches long, and disproportionately broad, but swims very swiftly, and is, for its size, as bold and voracious as the shark. When I said Mr. Meredith *did* not fish with a line and rod, I might have added that he *could* not, for the toad-fish, which swarm everywhere, no sooner see anything dropped in the water, than they dart towards it by dozens, and fight among themselves for the

honour of swallowing your hook, generally taking the precaution
to bite off the line at the same time. This extreme anxiety to be
caught might perhaps be pardoned were the greedy little wretches
fit to eat, but they are highly poisonous; and although I should
have thought their disgusting appearance sufficient to prevent
their being tried, I know one instance, at least, of their fatal
effects, a lady with whose family I am intimate having died in
consequence of eating them. As they thus effectually put a
stop to our angling, by biting off every hook dropped in the water
before any other fish had time to look at it, they especially enjoyed the benefit of the fishing-spear, upon which many hundreds,
if not thousands, must have been impaled in succession. This
sounds very wantonly cruel, I doubt not, but let no one pro-
nounce it so who is not well acquainted with toad-fish; from
those who are, I fear no reproof. When speared, they directly
inflate their leathery skins to the shape of a balloon, and eject
a stream of liquid from their mouths, with a report as if they had
burst. If flung again into the water, however wounded, they
instantly swim about and begin eating; and should one be a
little less active than his fellows, they forthwith attack and eat
him up. Even my poor little harmless friends the crabs become
their victims; when these usually well-armed troops have just
got their soft new coats on, and are almost defenceless, then
come the cowardly, ravenous toad-fish, and make terrible on-
slaughts among them—an attention which, I believe, the crabs
eventually repay with interest.

A tree which we, I know not if correctly, called the man-
grove, grew very luxuriantly on the brink of the salt-water all
along the embankments. Many of the trees, from their gnarled
and twisted appearance, seemed very old, but all were clothed in
a rich glossy verdure, something like the laurel, the leaves not
being quite so large.

In the too-completely cleared space around Homebush these
belts of green trees skirting the water were of great value in our
view, and the sailing boats which daily passed up the creek,
glancing behind and between the groups of mangroves, added
infinitely to our home-pictures, and served to build many a pleasant little fiction upon as they gaily glided past; distance rendering all blemishes invisible. After a time, however, these

" light barks" were stripped of half their interest and all their romance by an officious friend, who heartlessly remarked, when I one day pointed out a particularly nice effect of light and shade on the white sails of one, he " did not know before that Jones's *brick-boats* came up that creek !"

Twice a day too the Parramatta steamer puffed in sight, as she passed the mouth of the wide creek down which we looked towards the estuary. And with a telescope, on a Sunday morning, we could plainly see the carriages and pedestrians going to the new church at Kissing Point, on the opposite shore ; besides having a view of the half-way signal-staff; and on a still night hearing the drums beat at the Parramatta barracks. Thus, in our quiet retreat, " the contingent advantages" were almost as extraordinary as those which the inimitable Dick Swiveller discovered in the apartments of Mr. Brass. Often, when we have sauntered in the garden and veranda late in the evening, especially on a dark moonless night, I have listened for a long time to the wild tones and voices that rose from the forest and the marsh, whilst the wind, gently sweeping through the string-like foliage of the casuarina, made a soft flowing music in unison with them all. From the marsh arose the multitudinous, incessant gurgling, croaking chorus of the lesser frogs, with at intervals the deep sonorous *clop, clop,* of a great one, the Lablache of the small fry, whose note is extremely melodious and solemn withal, not unlike a single stroke on a very mellow musical bell. The long clear treble note of the shy curlew often came from many points at once, now near, now distant—calling and answering each other. Many persons dislike their cry, but to me it has a most plaintive, melodious tone, and sometimes the concluding cadence is far from melancholy. I often tried to see the curlews, but they retreat on the slightest sound or motion, and, except the tame ones at Parramatta, I only knew them as an airy voice heard in the " stilly night." The least pleasing part of our natural concert was that taken by the troops of dingoes, and unfortunately it was often the most prominent. Their indescribably wild and dismal yelling and howling seemed like the cries that evil and tortured spirits might utter in their dire agony, and often drove me within ; for though not usually a " nervous" person, they made me feel positively uncomfortable, and conjured

up all the fearful stories of ravenous wolves in howling wilder-
nesses, and packs of jackals, and all the natural-history-book horrors that I used to shudder over when a child.

Some of the vineyards and orange-groves near us were extensive and very beautiful. The large orange-trees, gay with their
golden fruit and exquisitely fragrant bridal-blossoms, are among
the noblest of all the acclimatized products here, and, with the
many other exotics common in every garden near Sydney, were
quite a delight to me to see. The handsome bushy pomegranate,
adorned with quantities of its large red fruit, is tempting in appearance, but its beauty is very deceptive. The rind is thick
and as hard as wood, containing nothing but seeds, each enve-
loped in a thin coat of acid astringent pulp; but the tree is always highly ornamental, with its rich glowing scarlet blossoms
and handsome foliage. The large-leaved magnolia-like loquat
is beautiful, whether laden with its pendent clusters of fragrant
blossoms or their succeeding bright amber fruit. The mandarin
orange is an elegant dwarf species, with fine, smooth, bitter fruit
the size of an Orleans plum. The lemons grown in this colony
resemble a Seville orange in their rough, deformed shape, although well flavoured. Huge bushes of the delicate oleander
are very common, and how lovely they are may well be imagined.
Geraniums of the old-fashioned kinds are almost like weeds, but
very few good varieties have reached the colony.

That magnificent indigenous flower the gigantic lily (*Doryan-
thes excelsa*) is often and easily cultivated in gardens, and well
deserves a place in the stateliest. From the centre of an immense group of long, broad, curving leaves the flower-stalk rises
to a height of fifteen or twenty feet, and of proportionate thickness, crowned with a great cluster of the gorgeous crimson lilies.
It is, truly, a colossal flower.*

Gardens in this neighbourhood might be small editions of

---

* The following little poem, written for a juvenile work (not yet completed), may perhaps be permitted a place here:—

THE GIGANTIC LILY.

Who loves to cull gay flowers?
  Come hither, all, to me;
I 'll show ye rare and strange ones,
  On grass and shrub and tree.

Do ye love the modest lilies,
  Each shrouded in its leaf,
And hanging down its gentle head
  As full of fear, or grief?

             I have

Paradise, had they sufficient and regular moisture; but the uncertainty of the seasons, and the impossibility (not to mention the expense) of supplying the deficiency by artificial means, render the most industrious and anxious attention to them a source of annoyance rather than pleasure. The *want of water* is a drawback of which no dweller in England can imagine the curse. I well remember my husband's admiration of our English rivers, brooks, and the little narrow, trickling lines of bright water that traverse our meadows and gardens; and when I used to laugh at so much good enthusiasm being thrown away on a *ditch*, he would say, " Ah! only wait until you have lived a few years in a *dry* country, and then you will better understand the inestimable value of such *ditches !*"

I have a lily here,
  A nobler one than those;
The tulip may not vie with it,
  Nor the dahlia, nor the rose.

Its long broad leaves are spread
  Down curving to the ground;
And I doubt if, as they grow,
  Four yards would span them round.

One stem from out the centre
  Of those bright leaves ascends;
As straight as is an arrow,
  It neither twists nor bends.

Month after month it higher grew,
  We watched it day by day,
Impatient to behold the flower
  In all its bright array.

It grew above the cottage eaves,
  Full fifteen feet in height,
Before one bud had shown a streak
  Of hidden treasure bright.

At length our wondering eyes beheld
  The tall stem richly crowned
With silken-petalled lilies, all
  In one bright cluster bound.

But not the pale and timid flowers
  Of northern climes are these;
Not shrinking from the temp'rate sun,
  Nor trembling in the breeze.

In robe of regal hues they 're drest,
  And to our fervid sky
With bold, unblenching gaze, is bent
  Each bright and glowing eye.

They scorn to share with humbler
    flowers
  Kind Nature's smile or tear,
And proudly above all their kin
  Their crowned heads uprear.

In lofty, solitary state
  They ope, and fade away;
Whilst far below, their scorned friends
  Dwell socially and gay.

The bright pomegranate's smiles re-
  The oleander's blush,   [flect
And roseate passion-flowers lend
  Pale clematis a flush.

The twining indigo enwreaths
  Full many a gentle flower,
That dwell together lovingly
  In some acacia bower.

The humble and the lowly, all
  Contented, happy, gay,
Laugh on, whilst in their lonely pomp
  The lilies fade away.

But think—how grand they are!
  How tall, and how arranged!
How far beyond those little bells
  That tremble in the shade!

Choose ye between the two—
  And then I 'll truly tell
If ye in lordly pride and pomp
  Or in happier love would dwell.

Our whole and sole dependence whilst at Homebush for a supply of water on the estate consisted of two or three holes, like old clay-pits, which were about half filled during heavy rains, and as no shade was near them, very rapidly evaporated in warm weather. At these the cattle and horses drank, and we had a water-cart to convey the daily supply to the house; but in the heats of summer these water-holes were completely dry, and then our unfortunate cattle and horses were driven three or four miles to another clay-pit, where we also sent the cart, with, of course, the constant fear lest, with so many claimants on its bounty (for all our neighbours were in as ill a plight as ourselves), even that source should fail us too. Some of our friends were at the same time sending five and eight miles for water, and *such* water! I did indeed then bethink me of the English meadow *ditches*, and how luxurious a draught their fair bright streamlets would afford. And as I commiserated our poor cows and oxen, parching amidst dry, brittle hay, for it were absurd to call it grass, without a chance of slaking their thirst till their daily toilsome pilgrimage along the dusty road, I used to think of the deep shady rivers at home, where I have seen whole herds stand in the summer noons with the rippling water often meeting over their sleek backs, and green, juicy herbage nodding at them from the bank, and such a world of luxury around as made the heat seem but a means for its enjoyment.

I would have all discontented grumblers in England, who growl alike at November fogs and April showers, and who always carry umbrellas by way of an implied reproach to the seasons of their native land—I would have all such sent to New South Wales on a " probation " system : let them enjoy sunshine, since they like it so much ; let them really luxuriate in a veritably " dry atmosphere " for a few years, and then see if their hydrophobia will not wonderfully abate!

When a winter rainy fit does assail the sky in this land of extremes, it certainly takes care to leave no doubt of its intentions,—for down comes such a thorough, right-earnest deluge, as not only washes away half your garden, but generally inundates the house, parched and warped as every part is by the previous baking process of the summer months. We enjoyed two visitations of this kind at Homebush, each of about a week's duration, and giving us the healthful advantage of an unexpected shower-bath in nearly every room. Every imaginable vessel was enlisted in the water-catching service; the tide in the clay-pits rose several feet, and our spirits in proportion ; but the old dry, exhausting weather soon returned.

A large well in front of the house, which had been closed over, excited our curiosity, for although we were told the water in it was salt, still, at so considerable an elevation, this seemed improbable, and we opened the well. To describe the anxious excitement which pervaded the assembled household as the first bucketfull was slowly drawn up, were impossible—perhaps Wilkie might have *painted* the scene, had he witnessed it : even our favourite old pointer stood wagging his tail, and pretending to lick his thirsty lips, as he by turns looked down into the well or wistfully into my face :—the housemaid ran for a cup that " Missis might taste first," but I was compelled to confess that the singular variety of unpleasant flavours the liquid combined left me quite in doubt whether it were salt or fresh.* Every one so ardently wished it fresh, that very daring anticipations were formed of the effect which the air might have on it, and various other possibilities ; but the experience of a week fully proved that our labour had been in vain. When poured into the trough, some of the pigs and one old horse used to drink the brackish water, but for aught else, save washing kitchen-floors, it was useless. The salt must have been derived from some saline beds in the soil, for the bottom of the well, though very deep, was far above the sea-level. Another half-closed well remained in one of the orchards, showing that every pains had been taken to find good water, but in vain.

After all my own grumblings at the climate of Sydney, which my impaired health and languid frame proved to be not without reason, I must give its two months of winter unqualified laudation, for then existence is no longer a burthen, nor walking exercise absolutely unpleasant. The early morning is often

---

* Some years since, Mr. Meredith and an old servant, being out together on some expedition, were seeking fresh water near the coast, for themselves and their horses, and after vainly trying the qualities of many small pools, God-bold dismounted to test another, but instantly began spitting out the water again with a sad wry face. " Is *that* fresh? " inquired my husband. " Fresh to *me*, Sir, for I never tasted any thing so bad before ! "

frosty, with a light white rime on the grass and a bracing sharp-
ness in the air, making a bright fire very good company at break-
fast-time. By nine o'clock the frost entirely vanishes, and a
warm sun and clear Italian sky tempt us to desert the fire and
sit by open windows, or ramble about without even an additional
shawl over a light morning dress. Towards evening we begin
to notice the darkness of the hearth, and a pile of blazing logs
merrily lights up the dining-room. In some houses grates and
Colonial coal are used as a luxury, but after being accustomed
to a cheerful, broad, good humoured-looking hearth of logs, they
seem to me very dull and sulky by comparison. The coal which
I have hitherto seen used is less bright itself and emits less
blaze than what we should term good coal in my native county
of Warwick. It comes, very appropriately, from Newcastle, on
the Hunter's River, a part of New South Wales I much wished
to visit, and had a land-journey been easy, might perhaps have
enjoyed the trip ; but to make a sea voyage, however short, for
pleasure, is an anomalous proceeding I cannot comprehend.

One great pleasure we enjoyed at this time, but have since
been wholly deprived of, was that of having plenty of books, as
we subscribed to the Australian Library in Sydney, and could
send for a fresh supply once or twice a week. We did not
obtain many new works of fiction, but of less fashionable literature, as Biographies, History, Travels, &c., we had abundance.
Neither were we by any means deficient in society, but, with a
few memorable exceptions, I soon found that Colonial ladies
seldom speak of aught besides dress, and domestic events and
troubles, " bad servants " being the staple topic. And most
gentlemen have their whole souls so felted up in wools, fleeces,
flocks, and stock, that I have often sat through a weary dinner
and evening of incessant talking, without hearing a single syllable on any other subject. Some of our friends had been among
the early adventurers who made the perilous overland journeys to
Adelaide, with large herds of cattle and sheep, and their narratives were always highly interesting, seeming like a romance,
often a most sad one too—after the dull wool-gatherings of more
every-day people. Far be it from me, in these slight remarks,
to imply want of respect for the worthy enthusiasts in wool ;
still there are times and places for everything. In English

M

society the lawyer does not carry his briefs and special pleadings
into the drawing-room; the physician dreams not of occupying
the attention of a dinner-party with his last wonderful cure;
even the author refrains from volunteering a recitation of his
new book; and surely, according to our old-world notions of
propriety, the wool-merchant also should sometimes divest himself of the " shop," and not be always encompassed and engrossed
by his bales and fleeces. However fascinating may be the company of his " fine-woolled sheep " and peerless breed of Merinos,
he should not insist on taking them out to dinner. I had to
endure a perpetuity of mutton in the wool; whilst choice
" samples," tied and labelled with most fond accuracy, were
passed from hand to hand, and contemplated with the profound
and critical air of a connoisseur passing judgment on a master-
piece of art. So long as the conversation conveyed intelligence
respecting different parts of the Colony, as connected with sheep-
farming or other occupations, I could derive amusement and
knowledge from it, but the eternity of wool, wool, wool—wearied
my very soul. Perhaps some excuse is admissible for this un-
social style of conversation in Colonial gentlemen, from the
rarity of Colonial ladies who are disposed to take a part in any
topic under discussion, and many, though not disposed or qualified
to express an opinion on general subjects, would feel insulted if
you asked their advice how to make butter or cure a ham; thus
rendering it difficult to know what they would like to talk about
when the servant-stories are exhausted, which usually prove
lengthy and very circumstantial.

I alluded to " bad servants" as being a constant source of
complaint amongst my friends, and I am well aware that in most
families the relative comfort or discomfort may pretty nearly
be proportioned to the scarcity or number of servant-women in
the establishment. Free women usually demand such exorbitant
wages, and are here such apt illustrations of the proverb, " Evil
communications corrupt good manners," that the generality of
married persons apply for prisoner-women to be assigned to their
service. Among these, a few prove willing, good servants, some
tolerable, many very middling, and the largest portion totally
unfit for a respectable place, not only from their inability to do
good, but from their inherent propensities to do evil, every

shape of vice and depravity seeming as familiar to them as the air they breathe. We were fortunate in having two decent emigrant families, the men as head farm-servants, and their wives and one daughter as cook, dairy-woman, and housemaid; being honest, sober, valuable servants, I was thus spared much of the annoyance suffered by others. I certainly had one very bad specimen in an old nurse, and who, although free at the time of her being recommended to me, had been doubly convicted formerly, and at the end of her five days' sojourn carried off with her several articles of value; for at that time I had not become accustomed to the vigilant care of my locks and keys, which is imperatively necessary here, and was, to me, extremely difficult to acquire. Having in various instances purchased experience somewhat dearly, I have since made considerable progress in this essential and troublesome accomplishment, and now as systematically lock my drawers, work-box, and other similar temptations, as if they were caskets of untold diamonds.

Wine or strong liquor of any kind is *never* safely left accessible to servants. The unlimited allowance of good beer common in English households is here scarcely credited, nor could such a custom be practised, for not a soul on the establishment would quit the barrel so long as any liquor remained in it. Tea, at every meal, is the Colonial kitchen beverage, with a good allowance of Cape wine on extraordinary occasions; but the quantity of meat eaten at least thrice a day may well compensate for the loss of beer. The fryingpan is in perpetual requisition, and seems to have scarcely time to cool between its performances; that, and a small iron pot in which the tea and coarse sugar are boiled together, form the sole cooking utensils of many a labourer's household: his bread is "damper," baked in the ashes, and varied occasionally by a "fat cake" done in the fryingpan, vegetables being rarely cared about. In stock-keepers' huts, and others where candles are not attainable, a light is procured by a bit of rag rolled up, stuck into an old cup or pannican full of dripping, and lighted. Home-made mould candles are generally used in houses where wax-lights are dispensed with, and certainly vary more in quality than any other article of domestic manufacture; but nothing beyond common care and attention is required to make them equally good with those sold by English chandlers.

Various circumstances having combined to determine us on quitting New South Wales, and permanently settling in Van Diemen's Land, we prepared for our removal thither, and in October, 1840, again returned to Sydney for a few days, which, as if to confirm my dislike of the place, and increase my joy at quitting it, were the most disagreeable I had ever passed there. The heat, even at that early period, was most oppressive, and the detestable mosquitoes (with their horrible allies) besieged us in swarms, cruelly tormenting my poor child, whose chubby face and fair fat arms were covered with their mountainous bites, despite of all my care and contrivances.

We embarked in a lumbering Colonial-built vessel named the *Sir George Arthur* (since wrecked off Bermuda), and once more passing the beautiful coves and bays of Port Jackson, sailed forth through its mighty gates on our way to a new home in Tasmania.

THE END.

London : Printed by WILLIAM CLOWES and SONS, Stamford Street.